Praise for *Valor*

"I was privileged and honored to lead US troops in combat in both Iraq and in Afghanistan and saw the best of them every day under the most demanding conditions in our military history. They were—they are—America's new Greatest Generation, and they were precious to me beyond words. I've heard the radio traffic of their close combat. I've stood next to their broken bodies as they desperately clung to life. I've walked innumerable sets of their honored remains onto the backs of our transport aircraft for the flight home to heartbroken families and a grieving nation. Sadly, little of the literature of these wars has celebrated the individual heroism of these young actors in their moments of truth . . . until now. In *Valor*, Mark Lee Greenblatt has honored this incredible service, and, in doing so, has performed a great service for America. In his words, crafted with marvelous eloquence, Mark has captured the raw, gut-wrenching emotion of battle and its aftermath in all its forms and thus has erected the ultimate monument to America's veterans, including the fallen, the wounded, and their precious families. We owe him, indeed all America owes him, a great debt of thanks."
—General John R. Allen, US Marine Corps (ret.)

"The stories in *Valor* capture very powerfully the extraordinary courage, selfless service, and sacrifice that our young men and women have demonstrated repeatedly in the wars of the post–9/11 period. *Valor*'s accounts of extraordinary heroism in Iraq and Afghanistan reinforce the increasingly widespread conviction—with which I strongly agree—that the young men and women who have served our country 'downrange' in the past decade truly are America's New Greatest Generation."
—General David H. Petraeus, US Army (ret.)

"Mark Greenblatt gives us a close-up view of the uncommon valor that is common among America's military today. . . . *Valor* is an eloquent tribute from someone who grew up hearing tales of Audie Murphy and the Second World War to the heroes of another Great Generation."

—Ambassador Paul Wolfowitz

"Greenblatt has shown [that] humility and valor seem to coincide when the stakes are mortal. Heroes don't only save lives and accomplish seemingly impossible feats at great risk to themselves—their stories can also inspire us to face lesser dangers and fears in our own lives."

—Brigadier General Howard T. Prince, II, US Army (ret.);
recipient of a Silver Star and two Purple Hearts;
University of Texas at Austin

VALOR

Unsung Heroes from Iraq, Afghanistan, and the Home Front

MARK LEE GREENBLATT

TAYLOR TRADE PUBLISHING

LANHAM • BOULDER • NEW YORK • TORONTO • PLYMOUTH, UK

Published by Taylor Trade Publishing
An imprint of Rowman & Littlefield
4501 Forbes Boulevard, Suite 200, Lanham, Maryland 20706
www.rowman.com

10 Thornbury Road, Plymouth PL6 7PP, United Kingdom

Distributed by NATIONAL BOOK NETWORK

British Library Cataloguing in Publication Information Available

Library of Congress Cataloging-in-Publication Data
Greenblatt, Mark Lee, 1973–
    Valor : unsung heroes from Iraq, Afghanistan, and the home front /
Mark Lee Greenblatt.
        pages cm
    ISBN 978-1-58979-952-3 (cloth : alk. paper) — ISBN 978-1-58979-
953-0 (electronic)
    1. Iraq War, 2003–2011—Biography. 2. Afghan War, 2001—Biography.
3. United States—Armed Forces—Biography. 4. Soldiers—United
States—Biography 5. Heroes—United States—Biography I. Title.
    DS79.766.A1G74 2014
    956.7044'34092273—dc23
                                                            2013047073

∞™ The paper used in this publication meets the minimum
requirements of American National Standard for Information
Sciences—Permanence of Paper for Printed Library Materials,
ANSI/NISO Z39.48-1992.

Printed in the United States of America

In memory of my mother, Marian Greenblatt.

Contents

Preface

This book tells true stories of brave Americans. As the country trudged through the peaks and valleys of the wars in Iraq and Afghanistan, I heard stories of extraordinary heroism by our troops—incidents in which men and women in uniform risked life and limb to save a comrade or accomplish a mission. I stood in awe of those men and women, frequently wondering whether I could muster the same strength, courage, and determination.

Over time, I grew frustrated that such stories—not to mention the heroes themselves—were not well known. I wanted to shout their stories from the rooftops. War heroes of previous generations, like Sergeant Alvin York of World War I and Audie Murphy of World War II, became household names, and cities and towns held ticker-tape parades in their honor.

We have no one like that today. Instead, accounts of bravery and self-sacrifice largely have gotten lost amidst the frenzied, and often nasty, debate surrounding the wars. Some are working to change that, such as the Jewish Institute for National Security Affairs, whose annual Grateful Nation Awards honor American troops for courageous acts. But the sad truth is that the few troops known throughout America are usually famous for dishonorable reasons or caught up in an unsavory controversy.

I finally became fed up and decided to do something about it. That was the start of *Valor*. In short, this generation does not have an Audie Murphy, and I set out to change that with this book.

Over five years, I sought out stories of courage and tracked down heroes. Learning about great stories was not terribly difficult; convincing a military hero to share his or her tale in a book, however, can be a Herculean effort. Many refused, citing an unwritten military code prohibiting anything perceived as self-aggrandizement.

Eventually, I enlisted—through an intricate combination of begging, pleading, and cajoling—a handful of individuals in my project. Their actions are breathtaking:

- a Navy SEAL who single-handedly liberated a group of Marines trapped in a house in Fallujah, Iraq, and dragged one injured Marine fifty yards down a dusty alley to safety as insurgents chased them;
- an Army pilot who landed his Apache helicopter in hostile territory to rescue two downed pilots, lugged one of them one hundred yards across an open field, and, because of a lack of space in the aircraft, strapped himself to the outside of the helicopter for the harrowing flight to the hospital;
- a Marine Corps private who carried a gravely injured comrade through close-range enemy fire from an insurgent-held building to a medevac helicopter roughly one hundred yards away;
- an Army Special Forces commander who fought back against a point-blank insurgent ambush armed with only a pistol and who ran through the kill-zone twice in an attempt to save a colleague's life and recover valuable equipment;
- an Army Ranger who ran across machine-gun cross fire deep in an Afghan valley and assaulted a Taliban bunker,

continuing his efforts even after realizing that he was completely alone and that his rifle had jammed;

- an Army private who, after helping evacuate several injured soldiers out of an insurgent stronghold in Iraq, gave CPR to a fallen comrade as a sniper shot him multiple times at point-blank range and then killed the sniper before passing out from blood loss;
- a Navy rescue swimmer who jumped into incredibly turbulent water in the middle of the night during a horrific storm to save a shipwrecked American;
- an Army specialist who held off an insurgent ambush of his remote outpost in Afghanistan, despite suffering serious injuries to his face; and
- a Marine gunnery sergeant who stood in a sniper's direct line of fire in order to help a close friend who had just been shot.

Each of the heroes received high commendations for their actions, including one Distinguished Service Cross, one Distinguished Flying Cross, and several Silver Stars and Bronze Star Medals with Valor Device.

But, beyond their obvious heroism, I grew enamored of them as people. Over the course of hours-long interviews and lengthy e-mail conversations, I saw that they were much more than guys with guns who had done brave things. As a result, this book is much more than just thrilling narratives of daring rescues and suicide missions. Instead, these stories explore a deeper side to these men, like telling of an Army Special Forces commander who admired an Afghan soldier and provides—to this day—financial support for the Afghan's family after the man died in his arms; a Ranger's love for his son, whom he calls "my little hero," and how he thought about him during an intense firefight; and a Marine who believed he would not survive a nasty battle in Iraq and thought about the promise he had made to his mother that he would return home in one piece.

I also tried to capture their humility, which is both heartfelt and powerful. All of them—each and every one of them—insist that they were not heroes at all. To a man, they say that they did what everyone else would have done and that they just happened to be in the right place at the right time. They typically deflected credit, pointing instead to the actions of a colleague, or attempted to downplay the bravery of their actions or the dangers they faced.

But facts are stubborn. And, in their cases, they add up to remarkable stories of bravery.

Acknowledgments

I could not have completed this project without help from a wide array of people. At the very beginning, Jeremy Berlin, a dear friend since nursery school, spent an inordinate amount of time editing my initial draft chapters and showing this attorney how to stop writing like a lawyer. West Point scholar Michael Matthews also provided invaluable help throughout my project, giving me a crash course on the psychology at play in life-threatening situations, putting me in touch with leaders in the field, and facilitating my search for additional stories. Bill Chatfield was indefatigable in his efforts to move this project forward, and his enthusiastic optimism was always an invigorating shot in the arm. As I told him countless times over the course of this project, he is a god among men.

Rick Rinehart, my editor at Rowman & Littlefield/Taylor Trade Publishing, believed in this project and took a chance on an unknown, unproven author. I will always remember the moment he told me that he wanted the book—"I'm going to offer you a contract," he said flippantly—as it ranks among the most important moments of my life. Assistant Editor Karie Simpson deftly guided me through the publication process and never bristled at my endless barrage of questions. I could not have asked for better partners than Rick, Karie, and the rest of the Rowman & Littlefield/Taylor Trade Publishing team.

My father, Marshal Greenblatt, and my wife, Jana, played integral roles throughout this project and deserve special recognition. My father read every word of every draft and offered detailed and insightful comments with each iteration. He has been a wellspring of optimism and support, which propped me up when prospects for this book were bleak. Jana has borne the brunt of this harebrained adventure since the beginning, cutting me all sorts of slack on daddy duty so I could write and not leaving me when I wanted to pour yet *more* time and energy into this project.

This book would not exist without the help of these people, and many others, such as Jill Chambers, Hilary Claggett, James J. Colbert, Dan Clare, Deanne Tate, and Tim Terry. My debt to all of them is incalculable.

In closing, I must take a moment to thank the heroes featured in this book. Not only were they willing to participate in a project with a guy who'd never published a word, but they also sat through extended interviews with me and answered every question I posed, no matter how personal or sensitive. Hearing their stories—both from the battlefield and from life in general—provided great perspective for me. It is no exaggeration to say that interacting with these men has changed my life profoundly and made me, I hope, a better person. I hope that my prose conveys just how special these individuals are. I also hope that my two boys grow up to be as honorable, grounded, hardworking, selfless, and patriotic as these men.

I must also acknowledge the men and women who volunteer to serve our country by joining the military, as well as their families, who bear tremendous burdens as a result. Their self-sacrifice is inspiring and deserves heartfelt appreciation from all Americans. The risks inherent in their decision to volunteer for service are evident in these stories and, while many of the brave men celebrated in this book survived the incidents described,

Chris Kyle, James Hassell, Christopher Alcozer, Nicholas Walsh, Ronald Payne Jr., and Afghan sergeant major Sumar did not live to see this book published. To honor their selflessness and express my deep-seated appreciation for their sacrifice, I will donate a portion of proceeds from this book to military and veterans' charities.

Mark Lee Greenblatt
Bethesda, Maryland
November 2013

Introduction
How Do They Do It?

What is bravery? How do people function well in life-threatening environments like combat? Why do some perform better in such circumstances than others?

Since the dawn of civilization, man has tried to understand the concepts of bravery and courage. Plato examined the virtue of bravery in a number of dialogues. In 350 BC, Aristotle offered intricate ruminations on bravery over several chapters in book 3 of the *Nicomachean Ethics*. Such analysis was not limited to Western philosophers—Confucius examined the ideal of courage, believing it was one of the three virtues of the princely man.

Only recently have scientists made headway in exploring the psychological underpinnings of these ideals. Research into the psychology at play in high-risk scenarios is by nature inexact. Examining emotions in such moments is particularly challenging, according to Brigadier General (retired) Thomas Kolditz, the former head of the Department of Behavioral Sciences and Leadership at West Point and a scholar on leadership in life-threatening situations. "Emotions are difficult to study and understand, [both] as they occur and after the fact," Kolditz explained in his book *In Extremis Leadership*. Likewise, Michael D. Matthews, a prominent military psychologist at West Point, noted that many of the relevant experiments are conducted in safe conditions rather than situations in which subjects recognize that they face extreme danger. For instance, researchers will start by asking the subjects to imagine their own deaths or write their own obituaries. Matthews noted the inherent limitations of such analysis: "I suspect that what happens in combat is much more real and may manifest itself differently than studies done with college sophomores."

Nevertheless, research is providing some clues about how the human mind operates in dire scenarios. Some studies indicate that individuals who excel in high-risk environments share certain characteristics. For instance, Matthews points to a study of recipients of the US Medal of Honor—the highest honor awarded for the American military—that identified consistent characteristics. The study found that Medal of Honor recipients have strong "self-regulation" mechanisms, meaning they exhibit "calm under fire." Matthews cautioned that this is not the proverbial calm under fire, "in the sense of having a lack of emotional or physical arousal." More precisely, he said, such individuals "are able, through training or natural talent, to maintain focus on the mission and put aside fear of their own safety for the sake of others."

This focus on others is another common characteristic of these exceptional individuals. Matthews called the trait "humility and selfless service." Kolditz examined similar themes in his study of leadership in high-risk—in extremis—environments, describing "the outward orientation and self-abrogation of in extremis leaders." Steven Abrams, a veteran who saw combat in Vietnam and currently treats combat veterans as a psychiatrist, noted that soldiers' commitment to one another can help drive them forward. "There is a collective group mentality that is very real," Abrams said.

Another interesting angle emerging from the research is the impact of training on individuals thrust into dangerous situations. The endless drills and simulation exercises establish a deep-seated foundation, so that combat troops can continue to function in life-threatening environments. Combat veterans regularly say that they switched into an "automatic" mode when things got ugly: they were not thinking through every action, but rather reflexively relying on their training to know what to do next. Abrams described a patient who was in the third wave of the American assault on D-day: "He had been so conditioned and just did what he was supposed to do, on automatic." That automatic response, according to Matthews, can be integral in navigating a life-threatening situation successfully. Such training and experience can empower soldiers to maintain focus on the objective, even in the direst of circumstances. Howard Prince, a retired brigadier general who received a truckload of medals for his performance in Vietnam and is now a prominent academic in the field of leadership, stated that precombat training "gives men confidence when they are scared to death."

Aside from the automatic response, combat veterans consistently say that they acted as they did because it was their only option. "If you reflect on the anecdotes of anyone who has faced death and is around to tell you about it, there is almost a universal response," said Abrams, the psychiatrist who treats combat veterans. "They did what they had to do. They never felt it was heroic, and never even felt it was a choice." Brigadier General Prince had a more colorful description of the concept: "When you have to do what you have to do, you do what you have to do because you have to do what you have to do."

Perhaps the most interesting discovery is that some people facing life-threatening situations actually perform *better*. Matthews pointed to highly trained professionals, like Special Forces or SWAT teams, as quintessential examples. High-risk challenges can "sharpen the way they think." Trained professionals in high-risk combat operations "won't even register a heightened heart rate." In contrast, Matthews said, "the way an untrained person would deal with that might involve soiling their pants."

Beyond common traits of individuals who excel in high-risk environments, research indicates that a strange paradox can emerge in life-threatening situations. Matthews, the West Point psychologist, described research establishing that "higher existential threat is often associated with an increased willingness to engage in life-threatening behaviors." Basically, when the situation is most dire, people may be willing to act in increasingly riskier ways. He pointed to one study that found that Israeli citizens have a stronger inclination and motivation to serve in the military when the perceived threat is high, even though the chances of being wounded or killed while serving in the military in such times are higher.

These themes—maintaining focus on the mission in the face of dire consequences, humility and selfless service, the paradox of risk-seeking behavior, and the automatic response imbued by countless drills—appear repeatedly over the pages of this book.

VALOR

Chris Choay on patrol in Kirkuk, Iraq, in the summer of 2003. Courtesy of
Chris Choay.

Chris Choay
"It Was the Loneliest Moment of My Life"

A rmy Ranger Chris Choay peered down the barrel of his rifle at the four Taliban fighters. He was poised to launch a surprise attack. They would be easy kills for the paratrooper, as they lay only sixty-five feet away. They had no idea he was there. If they simply looked to their left, Choay would be a dead man. He was completely exposed and severely outgunned; his one standard-issue rifle was no match for their three machine guns, not to mention the devastating rocket-propelled grenade launcher. But they were preoccupied with shooting at Choay's squad, eight other Rangers who were pinned down about 650 feet away across a rugged Afghan valley. Choay had used a flanking maneuver to sneak up beside the guerrillas. He was so close that, in the scope of his rifle, one of them "looked like he was sitting across a dining table from me." Choay drew in a breath and prepared to shoot.

And then disaster struck: his rifle jammed.

In the spring of 2005, the sentiment in Afghanistan was a curious mix of optimism tempered by caution. The previous year had seen improved security, as well as progress on political fronts.

1

The country adopted a new constitution in January 2004 and nine months later successfully staged a national election to select a president. Parliamentary and local elections were scheduled for September 2005. For months, US and Afghan officials had publicly predicted the demise of the Taliban insurgency. In April, for instance, a former commander of US forces in Afghanistan stated that the insurgency was in decline and anticipated that the Taliban would largely break apart over the next few months.

Nevertheless, the insurgents were simply not going away. Afghan villagers reported increased sightings of Taliban fighters in the spring of 2005. Taliban recruits were seen crossing over the border from Pakistan to join in guerrilla attacks on US forces. Insurgents had ambushed an American platoon on April 15 and engaged in a nasty firefight with US Special Forces on April 18. The US military reacted aggressively to all this activity, ramping up its efforts to snuff out insurgency and pacify the mountainous border regions.

By then, Choay and his unit had already spent more than a year in Afghanistan. A staff sergeant of the 503rd Infantry Regiment, 173rd Airborne Brigade, Choay was the leader of an eight-man machine-gun squad. "Our unit is known for a proud tradition and history of being parachutists." His men, he stated proudly, were "line dogs," a Vietnam-era term meaning infantry grunts—"the ones on the front line," Choay said. They had started their second tour in Afghanistan just a few weeks earlier, stationed at Forward Operating Base Lagman in the southeastern part of the country, about an hour north of Kandahar near the Pakistani border. Their mission was not just fighting the Taliban: "Going in, we had the knowledge that we will be dealing more with locals, civilian affairs efforts, and mainly focusing on helping the people with less gunpowder and more cement."

Nevertheless, these men were soldiers in a hostile environment, and they understood that combat was never far away. Choay felt that their predecessors became complacent and let their guard down, speaking incredulously about the death of an American soldier to an improvised explosive device (IED) placed at the main gate of the base. That kept them focused, believing that "the enemy will always be around the corner, waiting for the right time."

Choay, who parachuted into the northern frontier of Iraq during the opening salvos of the Iraq war in 2003, described differences between the combat in Iraq and in Afghanistan. "The Iraqi war was actually fun. I know it may sound weird, but it was," he said. "You see what you shoot. You [are] actually fighting visible combatants." Afghanistan was different, largely because of the setting. "You're fighting against them on top of terrains known only to mountain climbers and mountain goats," Choay said. "This is their backyard. We were ready for a fight, but more we were ready for a different type of fight, in a whole different terrain." Choay and his line dogs would experience that type of combat in a brutal, exhausting firefight in a rugged Afghan valley on May 3, 2005.

Choay was at the battalion headquarters at FOB Lagman when he learned that a handful of American troops were under intense fire in Baluc Kalay, a mountainous area to the northeast between Kabul and the Pakistani border. They were grossly outnumbered and desperately fending off the insurgent ambush. Choay's squad promptly gathered their gear and prepared to join the battle with another infantry squad and a four-man team. "I was ready and I was somewhat excited to go out," Choay said. "That is my nature during battles."

Then they waited for helicopters—CH-47 Chinooks—to fly them to the battle zone. The wait for the choppers was typical but, under the conditions, agonizing. The soldiers roasted in the 110-degree Afghan summer sun in full battle dress: thirty-five or forty pounds of gear (including vests, helmets, and ammunition), plus a sixty-five- to ninety-pound rucksack. Ironically, the only thing more agonizing than the heat was the breeze. "When it blew in your face," Choay explained, "it actually brought more humidity." But the worst part of all for Choay and his squad was waiting two hours, completely powerless to help fellow American soldiers who were under attack.

New to his role as squad leader, Choay's mind was racing. "I was asking questions to myself about all the worst scenarios you can imagine." He was also focused on "the hows and the wheres" of the mission: "How are we going to get to the enemy? And where are my Ranger buddies in relation to the enemy?" As Choay mulled over his options, however, the situation on the ground was fluid: "The intel kept changing every five minutes, and the status of the objective was getting worse." Envisioning the worst-case scenarios helped Choay plan: "I can see if we got everything. Did I forget to brief any angles?" Choay also thought about his men and decided against a Knute Rockne–style pep talk: "What can I say to these young men [who] are about to witness the biggest firefight in their lives? Nothing."

Nearly two hours after he first heard about the firefight in Baluc Kalay, Choay and his squad had boarded the choppers and were approaching the battle zone. Choay's unit traveled in one CH-47. A second helicopter carried the other units: a machine-gun squad comprising six men with two machine guns and a "headquarters" team composed of four men.

The helicopters were crammed with paratroopers and equipment. They knew they were heading toward a brutal fight. They brought enough gear to "to last us a whole lifetime." A sense of foreboding hung in the air. "The bird was packed with no sense of coming back."

As the helicopters approached the landing zone (the LZ), they learned that the situation on the ground had deteriorated dramatically. "We were notified that the LZ was 'hot,'" Choay recalled, meaning that the projected landing site was no longer safe because of enemy activity. "One Humvee [was] on fire, [and] the friendly forces on the ground had been pushed back. The place we were going to land [was] crowded with enemies."

But Choay was more concerned about incoming fire: "Landing in a battle zone is the great part. Flying in the battlefield is the hard part." The CH-47 carrying the other units received "effective fire," Choay's Spartan description of two rocket-propelled grenades that hit the other chopper. The helicopter sustained only moderate damage, however, and none of the Americans suffered injuries. The helicopter eventually touched down safely in an alternate LZ a short distance from the original site. Choay's CH-47, also diverted from the projected landing zone, set down safely in a nearby location. Choay and his unit hopped out.

The line dogs had arrived.

"I am the most outgoing person you will ever meet," Choay said. That sunny disposition springs from a deeply religious background. He was raised in an observant Catholic family that celebrates all sorts of Catholic holidays and "never misses a service on Sunday." He attended schools where students prayed twice a day. "I have no 'hates,' no disputes unsettled. I cherish what God gave me—friends, family, etc." Even this sunny outlook, however, had its limitations: "Hatred was nowhere to be found," Choay joked, "except when I skipped Sunday mass."

He is a natural athlete. He played football as a kid and does mixed martial arts to stay in shape. Standing five foot eight, Choay insists he is short, but in his relentlessly positive world, that is a good thing: "It's just enough to keep me away from attention."

Beyond his upbeat outlook and his religious background, two characteristics stand out. First, he adores his young son. Choay frequently mentions his son as an inspiration, calling him "my little hero."

He holds a similar reverence for his fellow soldiers. Any conversation with Christopher Choay concerning his military experiences is peppered with expressions of profound devotion to and admiration for his "brothers." His passion for his comrades—especially his beloved squad—is nothing short of palpable. Infantry squads like Choay's are supposed to have nine soldiers, featuring two three-man gun teams. But his unit was slightly undermanned, and he had to make do with a group of eight, broken into a three-man gun team (the alpha team), a two-man gun team (the bravo team), a grenadier, and a sniper.

Choay's squad of line dogs was close, enjoying the sort of trust that can be forged only during shared combat experience. Choay had fought with the alpha and bravo team leaders in multiple engagements, and two other squad members had parachuted into Iraq with him in 2003 to secure that country's northern front. The whole squad had also fought together in previous engagements in Afghanistan.

The others paratroopers tended to share Choay's can-do attitude. "A majority of the squad," Choay stated, "were on the same sheet of music." Although he readily called himself "aggressive," he shied away from the term when describing his squad. He was more nuanced in his description of its other members, preferring to focus on their adaptability and willingness to jump into the fray: "Our squad was the 'flexible' squad in the platoon," he said. "We were flexible to any mission regarding eliminating the bad guys."

The mission on May 3, 2005, would test that flexibility. That battle, Choay said, changed their lives forever.

As he disembarked from the helicopter, Choay surveyed the environment. They had landed on the high ground of a scraggly hill, facing northwest. In front of them stretched a small valley bracketed by another hill to the north. The slopes of the hills were uninviting—steep and rocky, littered with sparse trees. Between those barren cliffs lay a lush valley filled with orchards and long grass. A wide river sliced through the orchards, flowing from the northern slope southward, and a small stream cut across the valley, running from east to west. A handful of deserted buildings, which once formed a small village, sat lifelessly in the valley's orchards to the northwest.

A group of enemy fighters had established a stronghold in those orchards, behind an old stone wall. The thick canopy of trees, which ranged from five to eight feet high, provided crucial protection for the enemy. American Apache helicopters maneuvered in the valley, struggling to take out the bunker, but the dense tree cover rendered them largely ineffective. Indeed, the enemy hideout was so covered that the Americans could not determine how many Taliban fighters were there.

From their dug-in position deep in the valley, the enemy waged a ferocious battle, shooting upwards at the American forces. The insurgents had already inflicted some casualties among the Americans on the ground. The Rangers didn't have the luxury of a dense canopy and had to scramble for cover among the hills' barren cliffs. The only semblance of protection came from a few big rocks, some tall grass, and the occasional tree. Worse, a handful of enemy fighters had split off from the bunker and established a position on a ridgeline high on the valley's northern slope. That meant the American forces were largely exposed and taking fire from *two* enemy positions.

Upon landing, Choay's unit was directed to establish on the high ground of the southern hill to prevent the enemy from maneuvering or escaping. The squad quickly set up their weapons on a ridgeline due south of the enemy stronghold, which lay more than eight hundred feet down into the valley.

Over the next four-plus hours, in the suffocating heat of an Afghan afternoon, the soldiers engaged in a fierce firefight. Choay and his men saw their platoon leader take a shot in the helmet. It knocked him off his feet, but he was fine. "No scratch—nothing," Choay recalled. "Lucky bastard."

The fighting dragged on for hours and hours. Neither side gave an inch; neither side gained an advantage. "Everyone was playing the defensive game," Choay recalled. But that was a game the Americans could not afford to play. The situation—a bloody stalemate that saw the Americans taking casualties—gradually became untenable.

So Choay's squad of line dogs was ordered to charge the enemy bunker. "Someone has to get in and change the way the fighting had been going for hours," Choay said. "My squad was that squad." In an ominous move, the platoon's medic was sent to join Choay's team in the assault. Another infantry squad and the four-man headquarters unit would support Choay's nine-man squad from the rear.

The prospect of leading an offensive on an entrenched, well-hidden enemy position—a potential suicide mission—didn't faze Choay. "I wasn't shitting bricks," he said. "I was ready to get it over with." The enemy he saw in the valley below reminded him of the unshakable enemy he'd faced in Iraq, but he decided not to worry his squad unnecessarily. "I didn't tell the guys how dense, committed, and willing these guys are to kill us. Why tell them? They will find out. Besides, there is no time to talk about feelings."

Choay was motivated not only by the colleagues in his squad, but also by the other American soldiers who would come after him: "We were under intense fire. All we could do was move up and eliminate the threat," he said. "We [either] finish them now or the next set of brothers who comes by later will suffer the consequences." Determined to eliminate the threat to his unit and the other paratroopers, Choay led his line dogs down the steep slope toward the enemy bunker, into the thick of the firefight raging below.

As Choay's squad descended the barren hill, "bullets were zipping everywhere." They moved forward using standard tactics, in which half the unit provided suppressive fire as the other half advanced. They pressed on, advancing some 165 feet down the hill toward the enemy bunker without incurring any casualties.

Within a few minutes, they arrived at the river deep in the valley. The river was "pretty large," Choay recalled, stretching about 130 feet wide, with high banks on either side. The only way to get over the river was on a primitive bridge "made of who-knows-what kind of trees." Crossing the bridge would be dangerous, as the unit would be highly exposed and utterly defenseless as they swayed high above the river. But it was the only way to get where they were going.

So they started scurrying across the bridge. It was "very shaky," Choay recalled, swinging left and right and straining under the weight of nine men bearing heavy battle gear. "We were getting pinged by bullets," Choay remembered. "It made for a pretty long walk." Yet none of the bullets hit them. They crossed the river intact.

Back on terra firma, they continued to advance in the direction of the gunfire. They understood that the bunker was down in the streambed hundreds of feet ahead of them—two or three football fields, at least—but they were not certain of its precise location.

They eventually arrived at the lifeless Taliban village sitting in the valley. The village's buildings were simple huts with mud walls two feet thick. They were uniformly tan with small windows and doors. "The mud huts were connected together [such that] you couldn't tell where one family [started] and when the next [ended]," Choay recalled. "It looked like a whole bunch of Indian adobes connected to each other." For the moment, the village was completely desolate, and the unit passed through in an eerie silence.

As they descended farther into the valley, the soldiers remained exposed. "The grass and the walls of built-up rocks were the only cover and concealment we had," so the insurgents knew where they were. "The bullets were still being fired at us. Enemy forces on both sides of the valley were shooting into the valley. They were doing this because they knew Americans were down there and advancing toward their headquarters." Choay then added: "Those Americans were *us*—the nine of us."

Despite the volleys of gunfire, the unit continued pushing northward, in the general direction of the bunker. They had covered more than three hundred feet without anyone getting hit. But that wouldn't last long.

* * *

Roughly 650 feet out from the enemy bunker, Choay's squad paused to return heavy fire toward the insurgents. Choay moved next to the bravo machine gun, trying to give an extra hand to his undermanned team. He crouched next to the team's machine gunner, and the bravo assistant gunner leaped toward them, bringing a supply of ammunition. As he dove, a rocket-propelled grenade, or RPG, whizzed right next to Choay's head and sliced across the assistant gunner's right leg. "The actual RPG didn't [hit] him," Choay recalled, but the rocket's fin "took his inner thigh muscles out." The wound, according to Choay's formal report on the engagement, was "about the size of two fists put together." The injured man fell on top of Choay, writhing in pain. The platoon medic promptly started treating him.

With the bravo gun team down to one man, Choay pressed forward with the alpha team. They advanced for another 325 feet under a relentless onslaught from the enemy bunker. Choay recalled those moments vividly: "The fire was so intense that bullets were breaking trees and twigs all over us. There were branches that fell on me while I was moving. We could see the knee-high grass being plowed by bullets, looking like little bugs were running through it."

Amidst this barrage of gunfire, Choay and the three men in the alpha team believed they had finally spotted the enemy stronghold. Choay saw "a bunker-type mud house" 250 feet ahead of them. Then he saw a man duck into it. But they could not be sure that it was the enemy bunker. Their view was obscured by a thick stone wall and the orchards' dense canopy of trees. The cover was so thick that Choay couldn't determine who or what was there. "They were behind cover and concealment," Choay later wrote in his report, "that made it impossible for us to identify whether it was friendly or foes."

The units behind them, however, radioed the so-called three Ds—distance to the enemy, direction of the enemy, and description of the enemy—which confirmed that the hut directly in front of them was indeed the enemy stronghold. It was unclear how many enemy fighters were there, but the group estimated that the bunker had two or three machine guns.

Those guns were still trained on Choay and the alpha team, unleashing withering volleys of gunfire. As the squad proceeded toward the insurgent stronghold, an RPG hurtled through the air and exploded near the group. A piece of shrapnel rocketed squarely into the alpha team leader's jaw. "His whole front teeth got knocked out," Choay said, "blood pouring down his mouth." Yet the man swallowed the teeth and continued to fight.

Choay, however, had had enough. Two in his unit—two of *his* line dogs—had gotten hit. Worse, his squad was running out of ammunition. One gun team was down to about twenty-five rounds. "Looking into the eyes of my men, my brothers, and the ordeal that we were in," Choay explained, "I knew something had to be done. I knew that this fight was going to be over soon on one side—either our side or their side." He decided to raid the insurgents' bunker.

After the alpha team leader suffered the injury to his jaw, Choay continued to move forward with the two remaining alpha paratroopers. They took cover behind a small crest in the landscape, 150 feet away from the insurgents. Choay peeked around the crest and spotted four guerrillas. They were dug in behind a wall of stacked rocks. Three of them had machine guns; the fourth had an RPG. They were in their midtwenties, Choay recalled, and they were dressed in typical Afghan outfits, except that they were wearing "ammunition vests loaded with ammo." They were squarely focused on the other Americans in the valley: Choay's bravo gun team and the other American squads supporting Choay's team. Those units were directing enough firepower toward the bunker that the insurgents were distracted and had lost sight of Choay and the alpha team.

Peering over the crest, Choay noted with a sinking feeling the insurgents' skilled use of combat techniques. This was no ragtag gang of backwater villagers. These were experienced fighters who "had more time in combat than General Patton." Choay observed them "performing basic offensive tactics behind cover and concealment." More importantly, he believed "these men were the best I have ever seen at utilizing their weapons." They were "talking the guns," which meant the shooters were alternating, so that two of their weapons were firing at all times to produce a constant barrage of gunfire.

Despite the fighters' sound tactics, Choay identified a crucial weakness. "The enemy was so concentrated on taking the gun team out that they didn't have any situational awareness." Their left flank, he saw, was vulnerable.

Choay called out to the two alpha paratroopers and told them to follow him. He planned on swinging around to the right, taking an elongated half-moon route to approach the enemy bunker and ending up on the insurgents' unsecured left flank. In doing so, however, Choay would be crossing right between both sides' machine guns. From his perspective, the guerrillas lay ahead to the right and the American gun teams lay behind him, so his half-moon path to the far side of the guerrillas would take him directly through the field of battle—and the machine guns' ferocious cross fire.

As he got up to lead the flanking maneuver, something truly unusual happened to the rugged paratrooper: he became slightly emotional, choking up for a moment. It had been more than six hours since he first heard of the ambush, and there had been more than four hours of intense fighting. What's more, two of his men had already been wounded by near misses from the RPGs. "I had tears in my eyes when I got up the last time to flank the objective."

Choay quickly gathered himself and started out on the perilous flanking maneuver. He scurried through the underbrush of the valley floor, trying to stay as inconspicuous as possible. "I was in the line of fire from everyone," he recalled—his own men, the enemy stronghold, and the other insurgents dotted throughout the valley. Thankfully, the enemy remained focused on the other

American forces and did not appear to notice Choay's approach on their left. "My squad was still engaging the enemy," Choay explained, "and that helped keep the enemy's attention from me."

Choay continued to creep up on the enemy. He finally got to within sixty-five feet of the insurgents—he was an easy target for shooters of their ability. Choay stopped and prepared for the assault.

And that's when he realized he was all alone.

"I told my men to follow me, but it was so loud with all the explosions, shooting, and people yelling that no one heard me. I had no one there with me. They were all still back where I left them."

Choay remembered the moment as "the loneliest moment of my life. I was dead center in the middle of the objective, all alone. I was scared, and I was ready to die."

"I was completely exposed," he explained—none of the surrounding trees had survived the firefight's volleys of gunfire, and so Choay stood there essentially in broad daylight. "Here I am," he recalled, "so close to them, and not a single one was paying attention." If they had simply looked to their left, Choay would have been a dead man.

He knelt down and raised his rifle. It was an extremely delicate moment: if he missed or something else went wrong, he would be fighting at point-blank range against three machine guns and an RPG. He reverted back to his training, which instructed him to fire at the enemy farthest away first and then proceed one by one toward the closest. Starting with the farthest target was essential to keeping the element of surprise. "The reason for that is that you don't spook the rest of them," Choay explained. Also, if he shot the closest man, "the round might go through and hit a guy you're not ready to attack."

So Choay aimed at the farthest guerrilla. He was the one handling the RPG, the weapon that had injured Choay's alpha team leader and the bravo assistant gunner. Choay took a deep breath and prepared to shoot. He pulled the trigger.

The weapon jammed.

Hearing that failed click of the rifle was a horrifying moment for the paratrooper. He stood there, completely exposed and basically unarmed, "knowing that I [was] fucked." He was sure he was going to die.

Choay hurriedly shook the weapon to dislodge the jammed rounds and dropped out the spent magazine. He gathered himself and prepared to shoot once again. "I said a little prayer in my head," he recalled, "and loaded the weapon and aimed my weapon at the farthest guy's head." He pulled the trigger. The bullet hit the RPG operator in the head, killing him instantly. The other insurgents didn't hear the shot. They continued firing single-mindedly at Choay's unit deep in the valley.

Choay then aimed at the next farthest man, a machine gunner. Another head shot. The two remaining insurgents again didn't react. Choay pointed his rifle at the third man. A third shot to the head.

The fourth guerrilla quickly realized that the other guns had fallen silent. "The last guy stopped shooting and turned his head to the right to see what was going on, since all the other guys had stopped shooting," Choay said. "Then he turned his head to the left. As he was turning, I had my scope on him, and he turned right into my crosshairs. He was close. With the scope, he was so close that he looked like he was sitting across a dining table from me." Choay described the next shot coyly, saying: "Well, you know the rest."

Behind the dead guerrillas, directly in front of Choay, sat a mud bunker. He believed the hut held several insurgents—"the resupply element for the main effort." They had to be taken out. As Choay prepared to move forward, an enemy fighter darted out from the hut, holding an AK-47. Choay shot at the man, hitting him in the ribs. Wounded, the man continued running for some thirty feet. And then one of Choay's men shot him dead.

Choay scurried toward the bunker to see what was inside. But the opening of the hut faced south—directly in the line of one of Choay's gun teams, which were pounding the area with volleys of fire. To take out the insurgents in the bunker, he would—yet again—have to cross back into the field of his own men's fire. Choay would essentially have to cross a firing range during target practice for a second time.

He moved toward the opening anyway. "I didn't care," he explained. "It had to be cleared or we would all be killed." Choay was motivated by the very risks he faced. "I knew I was going to get hit, which made it easier for me to move. Accepting the worst-case scenarios seemed to help."

He dropped to the ground and crawled to duck under the gunfire peppering the air. The crawling was "nothing special," he said, "just enough to keep me from getting shot at." When there was a fleeting lull and the machine guns momentarily fell silent, he got up and sprinted for a stretch. Then it was back to crawling—"hands, elbows, and knees."

He finally arrived at the hut. Peering in the doorway, he "met the barrel of an AK-47 shooting at me from five feet away." Choay reacted quickly, falling backward and shooting back at the man as he emerged from the hut. Both shots missed. The man darted back into the bunker. Choay scampered a few feet away and threw a grenade into the hut. He heard frantic yelling inside the bunker. Then "the grenade went off, and no one said anything."

Choay entered the bunker to make sure it was cleared. Six insurgents lay there, with weapons and ammunition arrayed around them. "These were men who planned to kill us," Choay said, "and they had every asset they could think of to kill us and get away with it." But most were dead from Choay's grenade, and the others were suffering from serious injuries and severe shock.

With that, the battle was over. Choay and his squad of line dogs had accomplished their mission of raiding the insurgent stronghold and eliminating the threat.

But Choay wasn't done yet. Two of the guerrillas were still showing signs of life. In a moment of remarkable self-control, Choay dragged them out of the bunker and began to treat their injuries. These men had just waged a fierce fight, desperately trying to kill Choay and his beloved squad. And yet, once the battle was over, Choay did what he could to save their lives.

Helping those guerrillas, Choay admitted, was "hard—very hard." But he believed it actually helped his squad. "My men see me as the fired-up leader that wants action, trigger time, and most of all to do the 'fast' stuff. I think them watching me treating these men that I just got done throwing a grenade on forty-five minutes ago was awesome. It healed them, and I think it healed me too."

Estimates of how many enemy fighters were killed in the clash vary considerably. The US military reported that more than forty Taliban insurgents were killed and ten captured. One Afghan policeman was killed and five were wounded. No Americans were killed, although military officials indicated that six US soldiers suffered injuries. Aside from the injuries to Choay's men, one American lost a foot and another was hit in the legs. A third was shot through his abdomen. According to Choay, that man bled so much that it took blood from forty donors to stabilize him. He eventually survived.

After the firefight, Choay realized that his gun's misfire probably *saved* his life. The rifle had only four rounds left—two in the chamber and two in the magazine. Without the misfire, he would likely have used the four rounds to kill the guerrillas, leaving him unarmed and exposed within point-blank range of multiple machine gunners hiding in the bunker.

After he returned to his base, Choay sent an emotional e-mail to his family:

When the firefight was going on all I could think of was the fact that I will never be able to see my son grow up. I will not be able to see other things that we paratroopers fight for so hard, the happiness of our family. Those twenty minutes of hell were a turning point in everyone's lives that day. My fellow paratroopers executed to the best they could to preserve the happiness we all have in our lives. I will never complain again about simple things in life anymore. I now have a relationship with my guys that no one will understand. They did great and that's why I am here to talk about it.

My dear loved ones, I can say that I have seen the worst God has put on this planet. I am grateful to have been loved by you, cared by you, and most of all, part of a family I can call home. I know that you are praying for me every night and trying to think of great things about me so you won't have to be troubled. I am doing okay here and I am trying my best to keep your prayers in good use. I am doing my job and I am also trying to do my best so I get to see you all, especially my little hero. I cannot tell you how much happiness there is in me. I hope that you understand.

If tomorrow never comes, know that I am a happy man with or without me saying it to you in person. My son is my sole purpose in trying everyday to accomplish any task however it may occur. I am a proud father and a brother to fellow airborne rangers. I love you guys and hope all is well home. Give everyone my regards.

Love and Peace Always: Christopher Choay (Daddy)

Staff Sergeant Christopher Choay received the Silver Star for his bravery that day. He returned from Afghanistan in September 2008 and became a Ranger instructor. "Don't worry," he wrote in an e-mail. "I will try not to fail too many ☺."

James Hassell carrying a severely injured Marine through enemy fire during the Battle of Najaf on August 12, 2004. Photo by Lucian Read.

James Hassell

A Son's Promise

When James Hassell told his mother in the spring of 2003 that he had just enlisted in the Marine Corps, she was *furious*. She was patriotic and certainly believed in defending the country—she just didn't want her son to be the one to have to do it. "My mom is really overprotective," Hassell said. "Always has been." She had a very different vision for Hassell's future, and enlisting in the Marines did not fit in that picture. "She wanted me to go to college, and she wanted me to do so many things. I guess she couldn't understand why I would ever choose that path." But Hassell was convinced that he should become—that he was *destined to be*—a Marine.

Up to that point, Hassell was a popular, fun-loving high school athlete. He starred on his high school football team in Birmingham, Alabama, winning a handful of trophies and receiving attention from Division I college football recruiters. He had a wide circle of friends, which included kids of all backgrounds and interests. Looking back on those carefree days, Hassell painted a picture of a good kid with a healthy self-confidence. "I've always been comfortable with who I am. I didn't say, 'I've got to hang out with the popular kid.' I always said, 'I *am* the popular kid.'" He viewed his self-assurance as a source of strength, but he readily admitted that his charming swagger occasionally manifested itself as a rakish cockiness. "I was walking around like I was Tom Brady *in my first game*," he said, laughing at the memory. "That's just a part of who I am."

One day during Hassell's senior year in January 2003, he was scurrying around school avoiding his principal, who suspected him of perpetrating some teenage hijinks. Hassell ducked into the lunchroom, hoping to hide among the throngs of teenagers and faculty. As he furtively glanced over his shoulder for the bloodhound administrator, Hassell spotted a Marine recruiter who had an office in the school. He figured that would provide good cover and struck up a conversation with the recruiter. That whimsical decision would change Hassell's life.

Hassell had never really considered joining the Marines, or any other military service, for that matter. He had long admired the military and thought there was "something real awesome" about the way they carried out operations. "It was very exciting at that age," he said. "The things you see them doing on TV, you just are in awe. It's like 'Wow!'" But joining the military had never entered his mind. "It just wasn't a reality for me. I think the biggest reason is that no one in my family was in the military. I have an uncle who is a research scientist, and my father is an auto mechanic." More than that, however, the otherwise cocky high school athlete questioned whether he belonged in the military. "I just never saw myself doing that. I couldn't imagine being as *awesome* as those guys."

But then he stumbled into the recruiter, and they had a great conversation. The Marine invited Hassell to stop by his office later, and that one visit turned into multiple visits. The recruiter made the military accessible to the young man, and the notion of enlisting started to pique Hassell's interest. "I did a little research, and I understood what the Marine Corps was all about. I became a fan of the Marines." He learned about the Marine Corps's culture and its past. He loved the fact that the

Corps started in a Pennsylvania tavern in 1775, and he was enticed even further by Eleanor Roosevelt's famous quip about the USMC: "The Marines I have seen around the world have the cleanest bodies, the filthiest minds, the highest morale, and the lowest morals of any group of animals I have ever seen. Thank God for the United States Marine Corps!"

Hassell respected all of the branches of the military, but he started to believe that the Marine Corps was different. "It's the best of the best," he recalled thinking. "They had a certain swagger. You know when you're around a Marine. You can tell when you are around someone who has been in the military, but you can always tell a Marine even before they open their mouths."

From his conversations with the recruiter and his own research, it soon became clear to the young man: he had his mind set on becoming a Marine. "It was something I wanted to be a part of." Nothing else would do. "If you want to do something, you want to be the best. No one dreams of playing college football for Northwestern; everyone dreams of playing for the Alabamas and Auburns and Oklahomas. You want to be part of the best."

At the time he decided to enlist, the invasion of Iraq was under way, and Hassell knew he would be deployed and likely see combat. "Of course," he said, "that was the idea." He recalled that the recruiter tried to convince him to enlist in a noncombat assignment, like being a truck driver or a postal clerk in a combat support group. "I wasn't having it," Hassell recalled. "I told him: 'If I'm going to join the Marine Corps, then I'm going to do what the military does—I'm going to go fight for my country. I'm not going to join the military to drive a truck somewhere.'" Hassell respected those military support personnel, but, he said, "I wasn't going to join unless I could join infantry. In my mind, I wasn't going to be happy in the military unless I was the main attraction—unless I could be on the front lines and be a big part of what was going on."

So he started the process of enlisting in the United States Marine Corps infantry. As he progressed toward enlistment, he mentioned to his mother that he had talked to a recruiter. He wanted to see her reaction. She was not happy. He could tell that she would be upset—*very* upset—if he ended up enlisting. He nevertheless continued down the enlistment path, but decided to keep a low profile about it.

Once he had formally enlisted, however, he told her everything. And that was when she unleashed a torrent of anger at him. "She was so distraught and so upset and so afraid of what was going to happen to me," he recalled. "She was just *convinced* that I was going to die." His mother simply could not fathom that her son would enlist in the military during a war. Hassell tried to defend his decision, but eventually grew fed up with the argument. So he told her he wanted to go to war. "That's the *point*," he said.

That did not go over well.

"Are you my son?" she said in disbelief. "What *happened* to you? Are you *crazy*?!"

"This is what I *want* to do. I'm eighteen—I'm gonna do this. Either you can support me or just be quiet about it. It's already *done*. I've already signed up for it."

His mother continued to protest his decision. To calm her down, Hassell promised her that he would return home: "You need to trust me. Trust me that, no matter what happens, I'll do the right thing to make it back to you. I'm your son—you have to trust me. Trust me that I'll make it make home to my family. *I will be back home to you.*" His promise to return seemed to mollify her to some degree. "She really put a lot of stock in that promise," he recalled. "That was one promise she was counting on me to keep."

A few months later, only two months after his high school graduation, Hassell was on his way to basic training at Parris Island, South Carolina. Leaving his mother was difficult. "When I left for the recruiter's office with my bags packed," Hassell recalled, with his voice growing tender as he discussed his mother's distress, "she was crying the whole time. She was very upset. She couldn't even talk." His stepfather tried to help, reminding her that her son was now a man and she had to let him go. The entire experience, Hassell recalled, "put a strain on our relationship for a while." But he pressed forward and departed for boot camp.

Those thirteen weeks of basic training changed the young man's life. Boot camp, he explained, is not really about combat training; the purpose of basic training is to change the recruit and mold him or her into someone who can mentally and physically survive the *rigors* of combat. "It's about making you into a physically stronger, mentally tougher person."

And that process is grueling. "The first month and a half of boot camp," he said, "was the hardest thing I've ever done in my life." He describes those weeks as "really intense" and "shock and awe." Everything the recruits did—every drill, every step, every utterance—had to be executed with intensity. "Anytime we had to open our mouths, we had to *scream*—we had to *yell*." Beyond the sheer intensity of the training, Hassell started to view the world in a different light. "Everything you learn in boot camp makes you question everything you knew before you joined. You looked at the drill instructors like they're the first people you meet in a new society and they're teaching you about this whole new world."

Perhaps the most significant change was that everything centered on the *team*, not the individual. *Everything*, even going to the restroom, became a team concept. "You would never say, 'I want to go to the head,' because it's a team environment," Hassell said, explaining that using the first-person *I* was a cardinal sin. "Even if you want to go to the bathroom, the request was 'This recruit would like to . . .'" The countless drills and exercises reinforced the focus on the team over the individual. "We had to watch out for our brothers—the other recruits. You can't just worry about yourself. You have to become the same person, and you have to do everything as one. When everyone is working as a team, you don't want to be the guy that causes everyone to do extra push-ups. You start thinking about everyone, and not just yourself."

The team-first mentality had a profound impact on Hassell, particularly in light of the deteriorating situation in Iraq. During their basic training in the spring and summer of 2003, the invasion was over, but guerrilla warfare was unfolding rapidly. "The insurgency was getting out of control," he said. "It was pretty bad at that time. They were kidnapping people and they'd started the roadside bombs." Against that backdrop, the worst affront a drill instructor could say was "You are going to be one of those Marines that gets someone else killed." That would rattle Hassell and the other young recruits. "They wouldn't scare us with getting *ourselves* killed because, after a while, we didn't really fear that. What we feared was letting down our brothers. We didn't want to be the guy that gets one of your brothers killed. You know, I couldn't live with *that*. I can live with mistakes in Iraq, but I couldn't live with being the reason another Marine was killed. I could never face his parents or family."

He adapted the Marines' team-first ethic into a personal credo. "In life, you're part of the problem or you're part of the solution. I say that a lot. That's the bottom line. That's my philosophy. You have your drug dealers, gangbangers, who are part of the problem in this world. But then you have lawyers and doctors and Marines and soldiers and police—they're out there trying to be part of the solution. Everyone has a different life and different things that shape them, but if you want to get to the bottom of it, you can look at anyone in this world and you know that you're either part of the problem or part of the solution." The concept had been floating around in his mind for years, but it took the rigors of basic training to crystallize it into a driving philosophy. "I always kind of felt that—I just didn't understand how that would work until I joined the military. I guess I understood it more."

Upon graduating from basic training, Hassell felt an overwhelming sense of accomplishment. "I had been part of championship teams in football and other sports—I had been around a lot of success in high school. But when you compare the two, it's like the other stuff *doesn't even matter*. When I graduated from boot camp, I was in the best shape of my life, and I looked back on all the things I'd accomplished in boot camp and all the things that I'd learned, you just have this feeling that you're ready to take on the world and there is nothing that can stop you. I don't think I'll ever feel another feeling of accomplishment as significant as that one."

Even his mother was pleased. "I could tell that she was proud," he said, smiling at the memory of her beaming face at his graduation. "She could see the change. I was a different person to them and she could tell. She started to come around. She was proud that I had made the decision by myself and that it turned out so well."

In January 2004, shortly after graduating from boot camp, Hassell was assigned to First Battalion, Fourth Marine Regiment, Charlie Company, Third Platoon, in Camp Pendleton, California. He spoke of the unit with unbridled passion and pride. "Some units are just *special*. And I felt that my unit in Charlie Company back in 2004 was probably the best infantry platoon in Marine Corps *history*. I don't think there [has] ever been a platoon as good as that company."

He spoke reverentially about his noncommissioned officers, whom he called "awesome Marines." They pushed him, taught him, and molded him into a real Marine. Hassell quickly clarified that the process was not exactly fun. "They put us through hell," he said with a grimace. Every drill and action was conducted with an eye toward deployment and combat, which loomed just a few months away. "They made us suffer here so that when we got there, we were used to it, and we would be better equipped to deal with it." They also reinforced the team focus, and Hassell bought into the philosophy, determined to be part of the solution, not the problem.

At the same time, however, he couldn't completely suppress his rakish swagger. The kid who strutted around like a hall of famer in his first football game had similar moments as new Marine. "My confidence carried over to the military. I talked a little smack here and there," he confessed. His athletic prowess over the other guys in the unit caused him to get a bit cocky. "We knew each other; we played sports together—that's part of the reason I ran my mouth. We would play flag football sometimes, and I just felt like I was a man among boys. I was like LeBron James playing in high school," he said with a cocky, yet still charming, laugh. "I would say: 'God, didn't *any* of you guys play football?!'" Hassell's swagger wasn't limited to the football field. "I would walk around like I had a Medal of Honor," he said with a big self-deprecating chuckle. It was harmless trash talk in a testosterone-charged environment, but looking back on it, he realized it likely grated on others. "I guess that could be annoying for some people. There were a couple of times that my staff sergeant had to tell me to shut my piehole."

The unit was set to deploy to Iraq in May 2004, just four months after Hassell arrived at Camp Pendleton and one year after his high school graduation. Hassell and some of the guys "partied like rock stars" for a couple of days before their deployment and then set off for the Middle East.

Hassell's unit was stationed in Najaf, Iraq, which they lovingly called "the Naj." It was a busy, modern city, Hassell recalled, with traffic circles jammed with cars and mosques everywhere. "You could see the domes of the mosques—they're so tall. You could look around and see them from anywhere." Two mosques stand out in his mind, one with a large turquoise dome and another with a massive gold dome. "It was a really eerie place," Hassell recalled, noting that threats lurked throughout the city. "It was very dangerous," he said. "It even *looked* dangerous." Al-Qaeda insurgents were present, but the big threat was the Mahdi Army, which followed the radical anti-American cleric Muqtada al-Sadr. The Mahdi guerrillas and al-Qaeda, Hassell said, shared the same goal: "to kill American troops."

During the first few weeks, Hassell and his unit engaged enemy forces in only a handful of minor skirmishes—no real combat engagements. But several weeks into the deployment, they were sent to fend off an ongoing insurgent attack near a sacred cemetery in Najaf. When he arrived on the scene, Hassell was invigorated by the action. It felt like a video game. "At this point, I was thinking: 'This is awesome!' I was really immature. I thought I was *Rambo!*"

But as the firefight endured for hours and hours, going through the night and into the next day, Hassell would lose his puppy-dog enthusiasm for combat. He watched a close friend die in the firefight, shot by a distant sniper and dying almost instantly. Hassell, standing a matter of feet away, saw the life slip from his friend's body and felt powerless. "We all felt helpless. There was nothing we could do. It was one of the worst feelings I've ever had, and I never wanted to feel that way again."

The death of his close buddy had a huge impact on Hassell and opened his eyes to the gravity of the situation. "We had lost a couple of Marines up to that point. But I wasn't there. I heard about it, but I didn't see it. Once I saw him lying there dead . . . it really made everything *real* for me. That's when I felt like this could happen to *me*."

More importantly, he mourned the loss of a friend. "I was very, *very* sad. I mean, the type of depression that you can't really explain. It really hurt me deep down, in a place where I didn't even know existed. All I knew was that one of my friends was dead now," he recalled somberly. The pain was so acute for Hassell because they were incredibly close. "This wasn't my family, but he might as well have been because that's how we look at each other. We were a lot like a family. I knew his family. I knew his girl. I knew his plans . . . not anymore."

Losing his friend turned him into a different person. "That hurt me so bad that it took my feelings away." It deadened him, to some degree, flicking a switch that turned off his emotions. During moments like that, Hassell thought back to his promise to his mother that he would return home. "There were a lot of times in Iraq—a *lot* of times—that I wasn't sure I would be able to keep that promise. I really didn't think I was going to be able to keep that promise, and I just said to myself: 'Hopefully, one day, she can understand why I had to do this for me as a person.'"

Still early in his first deployment, just a few weeks after his friend's death, Hassell's unit was conducting raids on insurgent buildings in Najaf. As usual, they started at 5:00 a.m. Despite the early hour, the temperature was already scorching—more than 120 degrees. "It was *hot*," Hassell said, bristling at the memory. It was so hot that drinking from his canteen actually made things worse. "You have to drink the water because you have to stay hydrated. But even the water was hot. The water," he repeated incredulously, "was *hot*."

Over the ensuing seven hours, they raided several buildings, including a large abandoned hospital. It was arduous work, and the men were dragging. "Imagine going through an eight- or nine-story hospital building and going every floor and kicking down doors," Hassell said. "We were all tired. I don't think I've ever been as tired as I was that day. I can't even describe it."

At midday, Hassell's unit partnered with an Army Special Forces unit, along with a handful of Iraqi forces, to conduct joint raids on the strongholds of a prominent insurgent leader. The objective for Hassell's unit was the leader's residence, while the Army team and its Iraqi partners were supposed to root out his affiliates, who were holed up in an abandoned schoolhouse nearby.

Hassell's squad successfully seized its target, facing only mild resistance. But they soon learned that the other raiding team was in serious trouble. They heard on the radio that the Army and Iraqi units raiding the schoolhouse were taking heavy casualties and needed help. *Immediately.* "They were going to be in serious trouble if they didn't get help in a couple of minutes," Hassell recalled. "They couldn't wait for a quick-reaction force to be launched from the base—it would take too long to get there, and by that time, they would have either all been killed or taken hostage—and we all know how that plays out," silently referring to the grisly beheadings, mutilated bodies, and burnt corpses that haunted American troops. "With that in the back of our minds, the staff sergeant says: 'Let's get there right now. We're closest to them. Let's get there right now. Fuck the vehicles—we're going on foot.'" They were roughly a quarter mile away, so they assembled in a tactical formation and double-timed it, running straight for the schoolhouse.

Their route crossed through a typical Iraqi neighborhood. "It was *very* residential," Hassell recalled, with a mix of large two-story houses and smaller run-down homes lining either side of the street. As with most Iraqi residences, large, cheap metallic fences enclosed the homes and their small front lawns.

Roughly one hundred yards away from the target school-house, the Marines paused at an intersection to orchestrate their assault. One squad of Marines (comprising twelve men divided into two fire teams of six men each) was sent up the road to secure the entrance area, paving the way for the rest of the Marines to assault the insurgents inside the building. A second squad of twelve men, including Hassell, followed shortly after the first. Another squad remained at the intersection one hundred yards away from the target to provide security for the squads assaulting the building.

Hassell recalled the pale, dusty road in vivid detail, particularly how constricted it was. "It was a small, very narrow street," he recalled. "If one car was going one way and another was coming the other way, you could probably *barely* fit those two cars on the road." That, combined with the high, thick fences lining both sides of the street, made the street equivalent to a claustrophobic outdoor hallway.

They ran up the road in an orderly manner, using a tactic they called bounding forward. Each of the Marines was paired with a partner, and they alternated down the road under each other's cover fire—one of the partners would run for a short distance, duck behind something for protection, and then provide suppressive fire as his partner ran past him and found a covered position ahead.

As Hassell's squad bounded toward the school, they received fire from all around. Insurgents planted inside the schoolhouse were shooting down at the oncoming Marines, while others holed up in buildings lining the street were also targeting them. Enemy fire popped like firecrackers against the dusty surface of the street. "We proceeded down this alleyway, from which every nook, every cranny, every window, every shadow was shooting at us," said another Marine in Hassell's platoon, who ran up the alley ahead of Hassell. "It was just nonstop violence and mass chaos."

The Marines bounded through the insurgent fire toward the schoolhouse, a two-story building with a dull, uninspiring facade that was typical for Iraqi buildings. The Marine teams ahead of Hassell provided cover fire as the Army and Iraqi personnel evacuated the building. The sight was grim. The Army and Iraqi teams had taken awful casualties during the firefight, and the evacuation was largely a procession of dead and severely wounded bodies. Worse, as Hassell moved toward the building, still ten to twenty meters away down the street, he saw the Army team leader directing the evacuation gunned down by insurgent snipers.

When Hassell and his squad entered into the schoolhouse, the scene was chaotic. The first things he saw were trails of blood snaking down the hallway. "Imagine someone laying in a pool of blood and then being dragged to the next room, and you see the drag pattern from one room to the next room—like the scene of a horror movie or a crime scene," Hassell described. He would later learn that a group of Iraqi soldiers had bunched up at the school's entrance during the previous firefight and suffered heavy casualties. "They got butchered," Hassell stated bluntly. Debris, mostly gear from the wounded, was scattered around the floor, but the blood and blood trails dominated the scene. "It was something out of a Freddy Krueger movie."

The situation was bad and getting worse. By the time the Army and Iraqi casualties had been evacuated, the insurgents had established a defensible position in the second floor of the schoolhouse. From there, they were rolling grenades down the stairs to keep the Marines from coming up. They were also perched in a window facing the street, shooting and throwing grenades down at the Marines entering the building at the front door. With insurgents rolling grenades down the stairs and their escape route effectively blocked by the shooters in the front window, the Marines were trapped.

The other Marines, who were providing support from the intersection at the end of the road, had snipers and machine gunners targeting the insurgents in that window, trying to take them out and relieve the pressure on Hassell's trapped unit. But they simply could not clear the room from afar. And bombing the building was not an option, Hassell said. "They couldn't just blow up the building because there were Marines in there."

The Marines in the building tried to assess the situation and maintain security in case the insurgents attempted a counter-assault. They quickly spotted a Marine lying on the ground in a pool of blood. It was a guy in Hassell's platoon named Ryan Borgstrom. He served in a different squad from Hassell, but they had conducted countless training exercises together. They had never become particularly close, but as usual with Hassell, they had exchanged some good-natured ribbing along the way. "It's kind of like brothers," Hassell said. "You make fun of each other, but you still have that love." Borgstrom operated a squad automatic weapon, a ferocious machine gun commonly called a SAW, and had been holding security on the stairwell to prevent the insurgents from coming down the stairs. While he was there, an insurgent had rolled a grenade down the stairs. He tried to get out of the way, but the grenade detonated before he could even alert his mates to the danger.

The scene was ghastly. "There was blood everywhere," Hassell said, his voice straining at the memory. "I couldn't see anything but blood. There was *so much blood.*" Borgstrom's leg and lower abdomen, Hassell recalled, were "all peppered, like he had been hit with a lot of small, tiny bullets."

At first, Borgstrom was in shock, but that quickly gave way to pain. "I was screaming bloody murder because I was in agony," Borgstrom recalled. "My body felt like it was on fire."

The Marines called for a medevac helicopter to evacuate him to a hospital. The helicopter was circling above them in support of their mission, but could not land in the street—it was too narrow and the insurgents would easily hit the helicopter from their second-story perch. The closest it could land was the intersection where their support unit was located, roughly one hundred yards away at the end of the street.

The squad's medic, called the corpsman, quickly scanned the injured man's condition and gave a grim assessment. He told the group they did not have much time, as Ryan would bleed out and die very soon. "The corpsman did his best to bandage everything and keep everything intact until he got to a surgeon," Hassell recalled. "There was so much blood, and we couldn't stop the bleeding—that's why we had to get him out of there so fast." The corpsman said they needed to hold security where they were, put suppressive fire on the upstairs window to keep the snipers at bay, and give someone an opportunity to carry Borgstrom to the medevac team waiting down the street. That meant carrying a man in full combat gear one hundred yards down a narrow, enclosed street, with insurgent shooters perched in the second-floor window directly above them.

Hassell volunteered immediately. "There was no hesitation," Borgstrom recalled. "James looked at me, looked at everybody else in the room, and he said: 'Get him on my back now.'"

Hassell believed that, among the handful of men trapped in the building, he was the obvious choice to carry Ryan out. The task would require speed and strength. Ryan weighed roughly two hundred pounds, and they would have to leave his full battle gear on, including sixty pounds of bulletproof gear, to protect him from gunfire while they evacuated him. Worse, Hassell had to carry his own weapon and gear, as well as Ryan's extra ammunition. All of that added up to a heavy load.

Hassell was the strongest and fastest person in the platoon—he was LeBron James toying with the high schoolers, after all—so he believed he represented Ryan's best chance at survival. "Any one of the other guys would have tried to do it," Hassell insisted. "But I think, deep down, everybody knew that the only chance he really had was if it was me that took him out." This was not the boasting of the cocky, loudmouth kid strutting around the football field, but rather the forthright insight of a man who had committed to being part of the solution.

It was a unique chance for Hassell to do something to save an injured comrade. When his friend died in the cemetery, and in other situations in which his Marine buddies died from IEDs or sniper fire, Hassell was completely helpless. "There was nothing we could do," he said. But this was different—he was not helpless. "This time, I had more control. I wasn't going to let that happen to Ryan."

In volunteering to evacuate his injured comrade, Hassell understood the dangers involved. He also knew it was a long run, roughly the length of a football field. He knew they would be moving relatively slowly. And he knew that the two men would pose a large target for the snipers sitting at point-blank range. He thought about the difficulty of getting *into* the building amidst the gunfire—and that was by himself. "I almost didn't make it *without* him on my back. So that was what made me think that I wasn't going to make it *with* him," Hassell said. "Now I had to do what I just did when I barely made it, with a two-hundred-pound Marine on my back with all of his gear." To make matters worse, he was already exhausted from the seven hours of raids they had conducted that morning, not to mention the scorching heat.

"I knew our chances weren't good: there was a good chance that we were going to die," he said. "That's what I *thought*." What he *knew*, however, was that if he did not do it, his comrade would definitely die. "I had a choice: either you can stay here and watch him die and you'll probably live—" he said, and then immediately cut himself off before finishing the thought, "but would I even want to live if I could just sit here and watch another Marine die without even *trying*? What kind of life would I have?"

There really was no choice at all.

For a brief moment, as Hassell contemplated what he was about to do, a torrent of thoughts swirled in his mind. "You don't have a lot of time to sit back and analyze things." Nevertheless, "there were a lot of thoughts going through my head in a very short period of time."

"At that time, you just kind of accept the fact that whatever happens happens. It may sound weird, but I wasn't really scared at the time," he said. The death of his friend at the cemetery a couple of weeks earlier had desensitized him to any fear about his own mortality. More importantly, his focus was on his injured comrade. "I was more scared that I would make a mistake and get him killed. At that point, I am fully committed—I am committed to taking him out, committed to doing whatever it takes, to do whatever I can to save his life. I didn't know if what I was doing was going to save his life, but I wanted to give him a *chance*."

Hassell insisted that his focus was nothing special—that other Marines would think the same way. "One of the biggest fears any combat Marine has is failure. For most infantry Marines, if you told them that 'You're going to go in here and you're going to die, but while you're dying, you're going to save some lives and you're going to do a great job,' I think most of them would be okay with that. The fear wasn't *dying*," he emphasized. "The fear was that we wouldn't do a good job; we would let our country down; we would let our buddies—our *brothers*—down. That was the biggest fear—letting each other down. For the guys I know, it's always been about each other."

Hassell squatted down low and, with the help of the other Marines, hoisted Ryan on his back, lugging him like a huge, bulky backpack that was writhing in pain. "He was really heavy," Hassell said, comparing it to doing squats with extremely large weights. Ryan was in agony, screaming right in Hassell's ear. "He was screaming so loud I could feel his pain *myself*." Hassell struggled to hear the other Marines over Ryan's moaning, so he snapped at him: "Stop bitchin'—I'm tryin' to get you outta here!"

Hassell and the rest of the team prepared to race out of the building and down the street. He paused at the door as the other men gathered their gear and formed a makeshift caravan around Hassell and Ryan to protect them and provide suppressive fire on the upstairs window to repel insurgent snipers.

During that momentary pause, Hassell grew introspective. "I thought about my mom; I thought about my girlfriend; I thought about my life," he recalled. "I was thinking about the future, all the things that I wanted in my life, and I was just thinking at that very moment: 'It's over for me.'" He thought about the promise to his mother. "As I was standing there at the door with Ryan on my back, before they told me that they were ready to cover me, I was sitting there thinking that I told my mother: 'I'm gonna come back.' I thought about what she said: 'There are a lot of guys who make those promises and they don't come back.'"

Then he heard the order to move.

Hassell lumbered out into the street and the searing midday sun. They turned left and began the long run to the awaiting medevac unit. Insurgent volleys quickly erupted around Hassell, bursting like firecrackers at his feet. "I could see the sparks as the bullets hit the road, and I could hear the bullets popping off the road, and I could see the dirt coming up." He felt at least one grenade detonate somewhere on the road, but it missed him, and he kept on running.

His heart pounded in his chest, and sweat flowed into his eyes. He looked down at his feet to make sure that he did not trip and fall, which would certainly get both of them killed. He was also watching the rounds as they pinged off the road, and he darted left and right, zigzagging so they would not get hit.

As he trudged down the dusty street, time slowed down, and his senses grew cloudy. "With the grenade and all the firing, I think I went into some kind of shock or something. I didn't hear anything when I was running. Everything went quiet. I couldn't even hear Ryan screaming." It was not just his hearing. "I remember looking down the road and, every step I took, it just seemed like the road got longer and longer. It seemed like I would never get to the end of the road."

Although his senses were strangely blurred, his mind was sharp. "I had the ultimate focus. I was more focused in those few moments than I have ever been in my life. All I was focused on was holding him as tightly as I could and running as fast as I could," he said. "I never ran so fast. Under the circumstances, I had Michael Vick speed."

Still, he felt like he was running in slow motion. "It seemed like forever. It felt like three days," Hassell said. "I was very nervous about what was going to happen—I thought: 'This could be the last few seconds of my life.'"

Borgstrom was thinking the same thing. "When we were running, I was freaking out because I remember looking down at the ground and seeing the dust clouds shoot up by his feet from the rounds coming at us from the insurgents. And I thought for sure I was going to die," he recalled.

Borgstrom marvels at Hassell's effort. "It was incredible. I have never seen anyone run so fast in my life—especially with *so much weight*," Borgstrom recalled with reverence in his voice. "James was a very big man—he had his own weight, his gear, his weapon, and I was also a SAW gunner like him, so I had all my ammo, my weapon, and my gear, plus my own body weight. It was probably two hundred pounds he was carrying. And he was *sprinting* the whole way to the Humvees."

Jostling on Hassell's back, Borgstrom was in agony. "Once we got outside and he was full-on sprinting, I realized that his canteen was pushing right into my leg wound." The grenade explosion had sent a piece of shrapnel through his thigh, which was causing massive bleeding. The corpsman had bandaged his leg, Borgstrom recalled with a wince, but "it was still a significant wound, and the canteen was pushing on it. Every time he took a step or a leap, it just dug in and dug in and dug in, and it hurt like *hell*."

The run, Borgstrom recalled, felt like an eternity. "It was intense. It was just really scary. It was *very* scary. Throughout the whole experience, even getting blown up, the only time I thought or felt that I was going to die was that moment. Even getting blown up, I did not think I was going to die because I knew I had my brothers with me, I was being mended and taken care of, and everything was going to be okay. But that moment, when I was on his back and he was running me out of there, I felt like I was going to get hit in the back of the head with a round."

"It was like watching a movie," Borgstrom said. "Being on his back was like being in a theater watching *Black Hawk Down*, only I was living it—living it with James."

When they were about ten meters from the intersection where the medevac unit sat, Hassell could see one of his sergeants waving his arms and cheering him on. Hassell remembered thinking: "I'm almost there. I'm almost there." He approached the corner and angled his run to shorten the distance as much as possible.

Hassell finally reached the end of the road and turned the corner. He staggered behind a wall, safe from the insurgent snipers.

He had survived, unharmed.

A feeling of relief washed over him. "As soon as I turned that corner, I remember thinking: 'Oh my God—I made it. I made it.'" He was not sure whether Ryan would live, but he knew he had done his part—he had given Ryan a chance to survive. "I remember being instantly—*instantly*—proud of myself that I made it and being so happy. I felt like I had won the Super Bowl."

Borgstrom, through his pain, felt like he'd won the lottery. "I remember getting to the Humvee and thinking: 'Sweet God, I'm gonna be okay,'" he said. "James just saved my ass. I'm gonna be okay."

The medevac and support teams had a stretcher ready for Borgstrom, and Hassell placed him down as well as he could, given his exhaustion. When Ryan was safely on the stretcher, Hassell gave him a pat on the shoulder. He thought Ryan would likely die, as the wounded man seemed to waver in and out of consciousness. He briefly looked at Hassell, and then his eyes rolled back and his head nodded down. There was blood everywhere and his injuries were dire. "It was pretty intense. It was pretty messy," Hassell recalled. But Hassell tried to remain optimistic and prayed that God would let him live. He offered a few words of encouragement, saying: "Fight, Ryan. *Fight.*"

A few Marines hurried around the stretcher and carried Borgstrom to the medevac vehicle. The medics then took over, and Hassell turned back toward the schoolhouse. He looked around and saw that his teammates had already run back toward the schoolhouse—they were going back to finish the job. Hassell wanted to help his buddies, so once Ryan was safely in the hands of the medical unit, he darted off back down the road toward the school. "I ran right back what I just came through to get back in the building to get back with my guys."

The firefight continued for several more hours, lasting through the late afternoon. "We were out there for a while," Hassell said. "It wasn't a quick thing." But, with ferocious aerial support from two helicopters and a jet, the Marines eventually cleared the schoolhouse and other insurgent-held buildings nearby.

Roughly one week after the incident, *Newsweek* magazine published a large photograph taken by an embedded photographer in the moments before Hassell evacuated Ryan from the schoolhouse. It is a dramatic image, showing Hassell carrying Ryan on his back as the Marines prepare to dart out from the building. Hassell had not yet told his mother about his combat experiences, much less the evacuation incident. He had planned on calling his girlfriend and imploring her not to tell his mother about it—he didn't want her to worry unnecessarily. "I was still over there, and I had months to go."

But, before he had an opportunity to call his girlfriend, she showed his mother the *Newsweek* picture. Upon seeing the image, she was predictably distraught. "She saw what was actually happening and what I was going through," Hassell said. "She saw it firsthand in that photograph. She saw Ryan bleeding. When I finally called her, she just couldn't stop crying."

Despite her fears, Hassell would keep his promise and return home several months later. He called the return from deployment "the greatest day of my life." He beamed at the memory. "There were thousands of people lining the streets, throwing a party, clapping and cheering. There was a feeling of appreciation. Everything that we went through, people appreciated. It was a great feeling—probably the best feeling I've ever had."

At the base ceremony when they returned from deployment, the first person Hassell encountered was Ryan. "He was limping around and came up to me and gave me a hug. We hugged for a good thirty seconds," Hassell said. "He just said 'thank you.' Nothing else—no big speech or anything—just 'thank you.' I didn't know what to say because I didn't look at it like other people did. Somebody had to do it, so I just said: 'I'll do it.'" So Hassell deflected Ryan's gratitude and responded with a simple "It's good to be back." He asked how Ryan was doing, and his comrade said he was hanging in there. They agreed to grab a beer soon, and then Ryan pointed out where Hassell's girlfriend was standing.

For his actions in evacuating Borgstrom, Hassell was honored with a Navy Achievement Medal with Combat Distinguishing Device. Looking back on the evacuation, Hassell cited the incident as a defining moment in his life. "I never really imagined doing stuff like that. In that moment, I felt like a challenge arose and I stepped up to the plate in the ninth inning and I knocked one out of the park."

Following the incident, Hassell felt that he had arrived as a Marine and, more importantly, as a man. The older Marines who had been to Iraq before had always treated Hassell and the other new guys as unproven rookies. But not anymore. He recalled one particularly tough Marine who had already been through a tour in Iraq and never respected any of the rookies saying, "Damn, Hassell, that's good shit. They're definitely gonna put you up for a medal. That was badass." Another tough guy in the unit looked at him, and Hassell could sense the change. "I remember both of them—the way they looked at me—it was with admiration. I could feel it. It was just a really good feeling to have the guys that you look up to the whole time, looking up to you and saying: 'Good job. You did it.'" Hassell felt truly validated. "I remember feeling in that very moment: 'I am here. I am finally where I've always wanted to be.'"

Hassell grew philosophical and introspective when discussing his military experiences. "It was a *pleasure*," he said. "It was really a pleasure to have this country put their trust in me. That's the way I look at it. I think that is the way a lot of Marines look at it. We're saying 'thank you' to this country. America is the greatest power in the world and to be its *protector*? To me, that's the ultimate honor. I can't imagine any greater honor than being in the military and being able to serve this country. And on top of that, to be able to save a life and make a difference while you're in the military, that is the icing on the cake."

All told, his time in the Marines, particularly his deployments, clarified and crystallized his philosophy of being part of the solution, not part of the problem. "Going through what I went through—I've seen a lot of Marines get blown up or get killed—I had to watch that and I knew these guys, and you think that could have easily been you. You start to look at life and you start to question what is the meaning of life. 'What is the purpose of all of us being here? What is my purpose in life?' I started to try to understand life more. And then I guess I just figured it out: if you're not part of the solution, you're part of the problem."

Being a Marine and fighting for his country was Hassell's way of being part of the solution. "I think that, whatever the cost was for me," he said, "I can go to bed every night knowing that I made great decisions, that I wasn't a coward, that I fought for my country, and not only did I do that, I did a great job when I was there. I'm not that football-playing loudmouth from Alabama anymore. I have been through a lot more, I've grown a lot, and I've matured a lot. At least once in my life, I affected the world in a positive way. At least once, maybe not my entire life, but at least for a few years in my life, I took those years and I gave them to being part of the solution and not the problem."

Despite Hassell's evolution and maturity, his mother was still overprotective. "After two combat tours in Iraq as an infantry Marine, you would think she'd think I could take care of myself," he said with a smile. "You would be wrong."

On September 2, 2013, James Hassell collapsed suddenly in his home in California. He was pronounced brain dead at the hospital days later. He was only thirty years old. He is survived by his wife and young daughter.

Hearing about Hassell's death rattled Borgstrom. "I have no doubt that James was the only one who would have been able to successfully carry me out. I fully believe things happen for a reason and I have no doubt that it was his 'destiny' to carry me out. Everything lined up perfectly, and I can't help but have this feeling that, if he wasn't there and hadn't done what he did, I wouldn't have made it. I had significant internal injuries, I was bleeding out of the artery in my leg, and I can't help but ponder what would have happened if he wasn't there. Out of all the people that I've talked to over the years—my brothers and James himself—it was kind of determined that, if it wasn't for James, I would have been gone. I own that. I've said 'thank you' to him many times, and still never felt right, and when I heard of his death, it was beyond tragic to me. I lost not only a friend, but a brother, and it definitely hasn't sat right with me and it's not going to sit right for a long time. After speaking with his family and his wife and finally seeing his little girl for the first time, I'm going to try my damnedest to live life for the both of us. I love James and I miss him and I wish he was still here—whatever it takes, I am always going to be there for his family, as he was for me."

Mike Waltz on a mountainside overlooking Kora, a small town in Afghanistan's Tagab Valley, on April 27, 2006, the day before his team was ambushed. Courtesy of Mike Waltz.

Michael Waltz
The Cerebral Warrior
and the Friendly American

Every month, Mike Waltz wires a portion of his salary to a poor family in Afghanistan. He has been sending them money for five years, amounting to thousands upon thousands of dollars. He has never met them. He has never spoken with them. He doesn't even know their names. Likewise, the family doesn't know who sends the money. They just know it comes from "a friendly American."

Waltz prefers it that way. He doesn't seek attention, sharing his story only after the relentless prodding of a close friend. And that story reveals a true hero.

In 2006, Mike Waltz was playing a unique role in America's effort to establish a stable democracy in Afghanistan. In fact, Waltz was advancing that mission in two very different capacities—as an Army Special Forces captain fighting combat missions on the ground and as a civilian policy advisor at the highest levels of the Pentagon.

Waltz's military journey began in 1996, when he graduated from Virginia Military Institute. He went on to serve his four-year obligation to the Army, rising to the rank of captain. While on active duty, he was stationed abroad but never faced combat. Waltz eventually grew frustrated at the inaction, and even though he had always envisioned a career in the Army, decided to leave active duty in 2000 for the private sector.

Following the terrorist attacks on September 11, Waltz was recalled to active duty. This time, however, Waltz tried out for Army Special Forces. Competing to become one of the elite Green Berets was brutal. Years later, his face would scrunch up when thinking of the endless drills, which seemed designed to push the envelope of intensity and cruelty. Waltz recounted one drill in particular: trainers filled large duffel bags with sand and dirt, and the candidates—who already labored under heavy rucksacks and were exhausted from previous drills—had to carry the unwieldy sacks for miles, just in case they ever had to carry an injured comrade to safety. It was a nasty experience. After nearly two years of training—what many call the PhD in unconventional warfare—Waltz was accepted into the Special Forces and donned the beret.

Upon graduation, he was made a team leader in one of the Army's Special Forces units in the National Guard, which meant he commanded a team of twelve Special Forces soldiers trained in multiple specialties—intelligence, weapons, engineering, communications, and medicine. Waltz smiles broadly when he reflects on his 2006 team. "They all had strong personalities, strong opinions, and could be a handful," Waltz said wryly. "My job was to deal with our higher headquarters, get resources, provide these guys a broad vision and broad parameters, and let them go. An officer cannot lead these guys because of his rank. He has to earn their respect through his ability to do his job and then keep their respect."

And he did, said a senior enlisted soldier on Waltz's 2006 team. The soldier—the team's senior medic, who wanted to be identified only as "Brian"—said that the men understood that he was "a high-character type of guy" and "a model officer." While some officers made decisions based on advancing their careers rather than affecting the battlefield, "Mike was not like that," Brian said. "That's why we respect him as much as we do."

The team was widely regarded as one of the unit's best, largely due to the strength and experience of its senior sergeants. The team did not have a specialty, such as diving or mountain climbing, which was fine by them. "The parachuting, scuba diving, etc., are only a means to get to the objective, and they take up a lot of training time and money," Waltz said. "And we are not really using them in Iraq and Afghanistan. That stuff is sexy but not really relevant these days. What matters in my view is what you do in the face of the enemy, in dealing with the populace, and in gathering ground truth to understand what is going on in such a complex place as Afghanistan."

Waltz was intimately familiar with the complexities of Afghanistan from his civilian job, managing the Pentagon's counternarcotics policy for Afghanistan in the Office of the Assistant Secretary of Defense for Special Operations and Low-Intensity Conflicts. In that role, Waltz helped craft the US government's strategy to combat Afghanistan's opium trade and establish the Defense Department's programs to support the Drug Enforcement Administration and the Afghan counternarcotics police. As a senior policy maker, he regularly interacted with counterparts on the Joint Chiefs of Staff, in the State Department, and on the National Security Council. Handling the juxtaposition between his influential civilian position—weighing grand-scheme policy issues and hobnobbing with the highest-ranking leaders in the US government—and his military role, as a "lowly" junior officer in the tiniest Afghan towns, took a degree of maturity and mental dexterity.

By the time the Army activated his unit for deployment in 2005, Waltz was deeply invested in America's mission in Afghanistan. He had become an expert on US policy toward the country and the nature of the insurgent threat, which would later lay the foundation for his effectiveness as a commander on the ground. "He knew the cultural landscape, the history, the very complex political aspects of Afghanistan insurgency," Brian said. "He was very well informed about what was going on in the country and how to make an impact."

As a result, Waltz was very good at processing information and explaining events and conditions to his superiors. "Mike excelled at that," Brian explained, noting that the team had a running joke that Waltz always knew more details about events than had been reported in the news media. He worked hard at staying on top of current developments—even in the most isolated hinterlands. Brian recalled with a chuckle, "He always had a copy of *Foreign Affairs* or *The Economist* with him." But, the medic emphasizes, "He had more insight than those articles."

Although Waltz may have been "cerebral," as Brian puts it, he was no aloof professor. Brian said that Waltz pushed his team hard and insisted on a high operational tempo, meaning that they completed missions quickly and then started the next one right away. "He was indefatigable." Waltz's mantra, Brian said, was "Never let the enemy get the better of us." That meant more, however, than simply being aggressive on missions and winning on the battlefield. "We not only had to not let the enemy get the best of us. We had to outwit them. Mike was always thinking of this," Brian recalled. "Whether working with our Muslim counterparts to hand out Korans to win over skeptical village leaders or trying to lay the groundwork for a new base in the heart of bad-guy territory, his wheels were always turning."

Almost all of the team members already had at least one tour in Afghanistan under their belts and, in a time when nearly the entire Army was focused on Iraq, they were looking forward to getting back to their old stomping grounds. They liked the isolation and autonomy that were afforded to the special operations soldiers in the Afghan theater.

When he arrived in Afghanistan in January 2006 for his second mobilization, Waltz knew that the country had been relatively calm over the previous winter and expected the level of violence to increase quickly through the spring months. Waltz also understood from his Pentagon experience that the Taliban had been using the tribal areas of Pakistan to regroup and rearm since their defeat in 2001 and planned a big offensive to give European forces a bloody nose as NATO took charge of the effort in Afghanistan. In the previous few weeks, insurgent forces had started to flow from Pakistan back into Afghanistan for the so-called fighting season. That, Waltz explained, was entirely expected. Fighting abated during the frigid Afghan winters, so military activities traditionally accelerated as the weather improved in late March or early April. The spring of 2006 would prove to be no different, except that this year the Taliban dramatically ramped up the number and boldness of their attacks and began using the hallmark tools of the insurgency in Iraq—the IED and suicide bombers.

On April 27, 2006, Waltz and his team were dispatched to run patrols and disrupt possible insurgent activity in a small village called Kora in the Tagab Valley. The Tagab Valley is a part of the Shomali Plain, a storied plateau north of Kabul. It is a war-torn region, traversed over the centuries by the armies of Alexander the Great, the Persians, the British, and the Russians. Situated in southeastern Afghanistan only sixty kilometers from the Pakistan border, it was a traditional hotbed of insurgent activity and a staging area for attacks on Kabul.

The terrain in the region is largely dreary, with interminable stretches of desolation. "There are rocky, gray and tan mountains, scrub brush, nothing as far as the eye can see," Waltz described. But it wasn't completely barren. After driving for days and seeing nothing but steppes, Waltz said, "you'd crest over a hill or go around a mountain and there would be the most lush, beautiful green valley. We'd typically call them 'little greendoms.'"

Small Afghan villages sat in those greendoms, and while they looked beautiful from the crest of a mountain, they were logistical nightmares for US forces. "When you get down in them, they're a maze of irrigation ditches, rice paddies, wheat, and maize," Waltz said. Dusty, dried-out riverbeds, called wadis, typically crisscrossed these hamlets and could be anywhere from five to twenty feet deep, which made even a short jaunt a trying experience. Worse, the Afghans surround their homes with thick mud walls, further limiting the Americans' vision, communication, and mobility. The towns' paths—calling them roads would be overly charitable—were usually old goat trails. Some were paved, but they were "barely wide enough for a Toyota pickup truck . . . with the sides scraping," Waltz said with a chuckle. As a result, American forces would generally have to leave their armored vehicles at the outskirts of a town and conduct patrols on foot. "You can see something down [in a village] that you want to investigate," Waltz said, "and it could take half a day just to get down there."

Kora was one of those villages, a labyrinth of wadis, mud walls, ditches, and goat trails. Waltz's team arrived in the village on April 27, 2006. For this mission, like many previous operations, his team had been paired with an Afghan army reconnaissance squad, as well as a platoon of soldiers from another coalition country. It was a veritable UN delegation, with three to four different languages spoken at any one time and a handful of interpreters to facilitate communication. Although that presented significant operational difficulties, Waltz—ever the policy wonk—couldn't resist such golden opportunities to train coalition soldiers.

The team set up a base of operations at the village's police station. The building was a drab, squat, ramshackle structure that doubled as the village's elementary school. All of its windows were broken, and its walls were scarred with deep pockmarks from previous insurgent attacks. It was hardly an ideal command center, but it was perched on a ridge a few hundred meters from the center of the village and therefore offered a valuable view of the town. It was about as good as they could hope for in the Tagab Valley.

Waltz wanted to get a feel for the area, so he decided to lead a twenty-man team—half American and half Afghan—on a foot patrol through the town. Notably, the coalition soldiers declined to participate in the foot patrol and offered instead to overwatch the patrol from the safety of their vehicles on the ridge. The team set out from the police station/elementary school, leaving the rest of the coalition personnel behind. Those units were backup, but they were under strict orders: the village was a "no-fire zone," meaning that they were not supposed to fire in the direction of the coalition patrol, even if they observed combat activity. The point was to avoid casualties to coalition forces or innocent civilians.

Despite the reports of potential insurgent activity, Waltz wasn't particularly concerned about the patrol that morning. While Kora had been unfriendly to coalition forces in the past—in fact, insurgents had attacked coalition troops on every previous visit to the village—the town's adults were out in the streets like on any normal day, and its children were happily approaching the Americans as they walked through the town. Those were telltale signs, according to Waltz, that the town was probably safe at the moment. If there were a problem, like insurgents operating in the area or an IED planted in the streets, the villagers would know—and would stay far away from the Americans.

To prepare for the patrol, Waltz thought through his equipment options with his usual meticulousness. He ultimately opted for a "light load," meaning that he left some heavy combat gear behind. A number of factors resonated in his mind. First, he sensed the favorable atmosphere and didn't think all of his heavy combat gear would be necessary. In addition, he recognized the acrobatic nature of their mission—they'd be climbing up and down walls and in and out of ditches—so he selected his gear for mobility. Other, more pedestrian concerns also played a role: beyond his weaponry and ammunition, he had a radio, global positioning system, flashlight, and night-vision equipment—"at some point," Waltz explained, "you start running out of pockets."

The final straw in favor of the light load arose from his Pentagon background. Waltz understood that he and his fellow soldiers were the on-the-ground ambassadors of the American effort in Afghanistan, and he wanted to remain approachable to the Afghan civilians. Wearing high-tech equipment and full combat dress would conceal his body and mask his face, which would inhibit the very relationships that Waltz desperately sought to establish. "I didn't want to be a Terminator or a storm trooper," he said. With all that in mind, Waltz decided to leave behind his grenades, a few extra magazines of ammunition, and his helmet.

As the patrol weaved through the town, Waltz was all business. He was attuned to his surroundings, conducting "a constant mental calculus" of looking at vulnerabilities coming down the path and watching for escape routes in case an engagement erupted. A mound of rocks on the left, an alleyway to the right, a wall in the distance—everything got noticed.

Waltz chose a standard route for the patrol, called a cloverleaf. He divided his team of twenty men into two teams of ten men, each comprised six Afghans and four Americans. The teams then formed parallel single-file lines and walked down the center of town. Waltz explained that starting out with his entire team in the middle of the village was a "show of strength." Once they reached the far edge of town, they split away from each other in elongated half-moon routes in opposite directions, forming a cloverleaf pattern. Waltz's team broke to the right (south), while the other team went left (north). It was integral, Waltz explained, that the teams go in opposite directions, so that they were not facing each other: "We wanted to be back-to-back facing away from each other—if we had to engage [with the enemy] and we didn't want to be shooting and hit the other coalition team."

As the teams proceeded through Kora, the team maneuvered through the village's labyrinth, climbing in and out of wadis and scaling up and down walls. Weighed down with sixty pounds of gear each, their progress was slow and methodical. Although the town was small, the patrol took two hours. They were exhausted,

Waltz recalled, but the patrol had been successful, and they did not see anything to suggest significant insurgent activity.

As the team regrouped at the police station after that morning's patrol, they observed flashes of light emanating from the ridgelines on one side of the valley and responsive flickers coming from the other. The team believed insurgents were using mirrors or flashlights to send signals to other insurgents about activity in the valley below—like the presence of American forces in Kora. The sergeant major of the Afghan reconnaissance squad, an impressive soldier named Sumar, suggested to Waltz that the team send a patrol up the mountainside to investigate the signaling. Waltz agreed—he wasn't terribly optimistic that they would find anything of interest, but he figured it was a good opportunity for a joint training mission with the Afghan soldiers.

Waltz and Sergeant Major Sumar organized a small team and led the men on a trek up the valley wall. It was hard work, walking straight uphill through scraggly terrain, weighed down with heavy gear. Midway up the climb, the men took a break to get their bearings and rest their legs.

Standing on a large rock and looking down at the sprawling valley below, Waltz started a conversation with Sumar. Waltz had gotten to know the sergeant major over the previous month, as their teams had conducted a handful of joint missions similar to the patrol through Kora. Even though Waltz barely knew the man and had seen him just a few times, he'd developed tremendous respect for him. "He really stood out," Waltz said. "He really made an impression on me."

The Afghan was a towering figure. He stood over six feet and weighed more than two hundred pounds, which made him a giant compared to most of his countrymen. Waltz believed he was twenty-nine or thirty years old, but the man's weathered skin and traditional Afghan beard made him appear at least a decade older than that. He was somewhat quiet, but not to the point of seeming aloof or dispassionate. That taciturn disposition, combined with his imposing physical presence, created a powerful impression. "He had an air about him," Waltz explained, adding that "you could tell his men respected him."

Waltz respected him too. He recognized that Sumar was a rare breed: "What stood out to me was that he was one of the few soldiers in Afghanistan—and frankly throughout the Third World—who acted like a noncommissioned officer as we would expect in the West." This was high praise from Waltz. He grew passionate in explaining just how valuable noncommissioned officers—called NCOs—can be: "NCOs are the backbone—*the foundation*—that the rest of the military is built on." While a unit's officers deal with broader strategic matters, Waltz said, "the NCOs are the doers. They are the directors where the rubber meets the road. NCOs are the guys that really make things happen."

Sergeant Major Sumar was one of those guys. He was a natural leader, Waltz said, taking charge because he had the experience to know what needed to be done and had the personal motivation to do it. What most impressed Waltz about Sumar was that he led by example. Waltz explained that unit leaders like officers and NCOs in American and other Western armies share risk with their men. That means leading patrols from the front—one of the unit's most exposed positions. In Waltz's experience, armies in less developed countries were quite different: higher rank meant more stature—and *less* risk. "As you get promoted," he said, "you stay in the rear. You stay in your office, and send out your underlings to conduct missions." Sumar was different—on patrols, he would be at the front of the unit, sharing risk with his subordinates. Waltz recalled with unmistakable distaste that the Afghan lieutenant who outranked the sergeant major would normally take a backseat on patrols, stay hidden in the middle of the pack, or just not go at all.

Sumar also impressed Waltz because he was proactive. Before operations, the sergeant major would take it upon himself to check the unit, making sure that they had water, that their guns were clean, and that they had sufficient ammunition. He would talk with the unit to ensure that they understood the mission: where they were going and what their objectives were. He embraced their broader mission and offered ideas to his superiors, such as the brutal trek that morning up the valley wall to investigate the light flashes. In the US Army, this would be standard fare for an NCO, but in the Third World, Waltz said, it was rare indeed.

Discussions with Sumar were always illuminating for Waltz, so he didn't pass up the opportunity during their break to strike up another conversation. Talking with the Afghan was easy, despite the fact that he knew little English. Most conversations with Afghan soldiers were stilted because they had to use an interpreter. Waltz noted that most people in such conversations speak not to the other person in the dialogue, but rather to the interpreter. That strained the flow of discussion and hampered the personal connection that would normally develop over the course of a conversation. But Sumar was different. Waltz recalled that he "had a natural ability to speak directly to you, and not the interpreter." Waltz found that habit especially endearing and tried hard to emulate it.

Years later, Waltz would remember his conversation with the sergeant major on the rock that afternoon. It was enlightening, as usual. The two warriors shared stories of their families, with Waltz chatting about his young daughter in the suburbs of Washington, D.C., and Sumar describing his beloved wife and six children in the outskirts of Jalalabad. Waltz inquired why he was willing to risk so much to fight against the insurgents. Sumar described his upbringing, particularly how his father desperately wanted a better life for him. His father emphasized the importance of education and worked tirelessly to keep him out of the madrassas, the religious schools that offer poor young Afghan boys free room and board as part of their education, but that are often manipulated to indoctrinate students in Islamic fundamentalism. His father understood that the madrassas were a dead end. The sergeant major grew emotional as he told Waltz about his own desire that his boys have better lives than his, which meant avoiding the fundamentalist schools at all costs.

Waltz listened intently. He knew these insights about one man were in reality a microcosm of the entire war. Winning over men like Sumar would be a massive step toward winning the war in Afghanistan.

Although he could have talked with Sumar forever, Waltz knew their respite was running too long. He and the sergeant major promptly roused the men, and they continued the hike up the mountainside. They eventually made it to the top of the slope, but found no evidence of insurgent activity. They walked back down the valley and made it down to their base at the police station without incident.

As the afternoon turned to dusk, Waltz prepared for the next day's activities, particularly morning and afternoon patrols through the town. That night, the team went to sleep in makeshift bunks in the police station.

When they awoke the next morning, April 28, the atmosphere in Kora was markedly different. Waltz sensed a tension in the air as the villagers who were so friendly the day before now kept a distance. Groups of men watched the soldiers, straight-faced and noticeably inhospitable. "There was an eerie stillness," Brian the senior medic recalled. "It was highly unusual for Afghans to be so unfriendly."

The most alarming change involved the kids. The day before, like on most other days, the kids were thrilled to see American troops. Many times the kids would mob the Americans as they walked through a town. And the soldiers basked in their affection, doling out candy, money, food, and anything else they had on hand. The most treasured gifts, however, were pens and pencils. Most Afghan schools, Waltz explained, had no desks, books, paper, or pencils. So the kids had to learn by rote memorization. "Having a pencil was a sign that they'd made it." With that in mind, Waltz and his team made it a point to hand out boxes of pencils and pens at every opportunity. Years later, Waltz remembered the kids' sheer joy in receiving a simple writing utensil: "You'd see these kids in snow-encrusted mud, standing there barefoot, and you give them a pen and they're beaming with a smile across their face. It was phenomenal," Waltz said, smiling broadly at the memory. "It really gets under your skin and touches your heart."

But the kids in Kora on the morning of April 28, 2006, weren't mobbing the troops or lunging gleefully at pens or candy. To the contrary, there were no children in the streets. Everyone understood that was a significant red flag that something might be afoot. "The town was bad," Brian said, "and we knew it going in."

At the same time, they had seen comparable red flags on dozens of other occasions and nothing had ever happened. More importantly, their mission was to ferret out insurgent activity, so Waltz stuck to the plan laid out the night before—a patrol through the village in the morning and another in the afternoon.

Just after daybreak, Waltz took a twenty-man team on a patrol through the town. They trudged through goat trails, scaled compound walls, and climbed in and out of dried streambeds. Red flags notwithstanding, the patrol that morning went off without a hitch, and the men returned to the police station to rest before the afternoon patrol.

After the morning patrol, Waltz met with several of the town's leaders and planned for the patrol later that day. Around 4:00, he moved out in the twenty-man team for the day's second patrol. Waltz opted again to carry a light load—only a few magazines of extra ammunition, with no grenades or helmet.

The afternoon patrol started much like the previous two patrols through the town. Waltz again instructed the team to follow the cloverleaf pattern. The twenty-man group was divided into two ten-man teams, which proceeded in parallel lines through the village. Waltz's team had three other Americans (including Brian), an interpreter, and five Afghan soldiers, including Sergeant Major Sumar and the Afghan lieutenant. Midway through the patrol, the lines split in opposite directions; Waltz's line broke to the right and the other went left.

About an hour into the mission, Waltz's team took a much-needed break. "We rested there on uncut grass," Brian later wrote to his family, "with birds chirping all around and the scent of eucalyptus in the breeze." Despite the relaxing and perhaps idyllic respite, their circumstances would not remain so favorable. The daylight had dimmed over the course of the patrol, and the surrounding mountains were starting to cast long shadows over the village. Those dusk hours were precarious times for coalition teams because the Afghans generally had no night-vision equipment, which made them nervous about nighttime missions. And it was not much better for the Americans, because it was too dark to see much with their eyes, but too light for the night-vision gear to help.

Waltz conferred with the Afghan lieutenant and Sergeant Major Sumar about their next steps. Waltz and the Afghan lieutenant had a heated disagreement over deciding the best path back to their base, but Waltz eventually persuaded the Afghan officer to not use the same route they had just used and to circle back through a large wadi on the south side of town. They gathered the team together to resume the patrol as the sunlight dimmed even further. It took a few minutes to get to the wadi, and then they started walking down the dusty riverbed back through the town.

Waltz started to get an uneasy feeling as they proceeded down the wadi. As usual, he was evaluating the environment, mentally processing vulnerabilities and options, and the situation was not promising. Dense, foreboding walls hugged the sides of the riverbed, giving it the claustrophobic feel of a tunnel. Rocks, thorny scrub brush, and sparse trees dotted the narrow passage and limited their mobility even further. Waltz quickly realized that the team had very little space to maneuver and few options if they had contact with the enemy. There were no easy exits from the wadi and few sources of cover. He was well aware that an ambush could lie around any corner, and he was getting increasingly nervous. "My Spidey sense was tingling," he recalled.

The eerie stillness that Brian had sensed earlier was getting worse. "By now, everything was completely silent," he said. "Nobody was out and it was as if the place were abruptly drained of its population."

Waltz knew his patrol team had to be vigilant and keep their eyes open. But the Afghan soldiers were getting skittish. They had been patrolling throughout the town for hours, so they were tired and hungry. Light was dimming as the day turned to night. Waltz could see that the Afghans on the patrol were not paying attention—they sensed the danger and just wanted to go back to the base as fast as possible. The longer they were on the patrol, the greater the chance of an attack. So they were basically in a walking sprint to get back to safety.

In their haste, they were neglecting their basic responsibility: patrolling the town. Rather than casting a watchful eye over the town to spot suspicious activity, "they had tunnel vision," Waltz recalled with palpable exasperation. They just wanted to get it over with, and that was exactly what Waltz was concerned about. That, he said, is how mistakes happen.

As the leader of the team, he knew he had to refocus them back to the task at hand. He beckoned the team's interpreter to him and asked him to call ahead to the Afghan officer. "Tell the lieutenant to slow down," Waltz told the interpreter. "This is a dangerous area."

Waltz remembered what happened next with remarkable clarity. He looked up and saw Sergeant Major Sumar, who was in his customary position: leading the team from the front. Waltz always placed the interpreter between him and the Afghan lieutenant, and, as the three of them bunched up to relay

Waltz's strong suggestion that the patrol slow down, Waltz saw Sumar turn back in response to a short command from the lieutenant. As Sumar turned back toward him, Waltz recalled that he heard the unmistakable sound of someone chambering a bullet. It was a loud, jarring noise of metal clanging. Then all hell seemed to break loose as machine-gun fire burst throughout the riverbed. He saw Sumar drop to the ground. Brian saw the first three Afghans in the patrol fall "like human dominoes."

Waltz's Spidey sense was right—they were being ambushed.

Standing in the middle of the wadi, Waltz felt a stream of bullets pop next to his head. The fire was shockingly loud. "It was like the D-day scene in *Saving Private Ryan*," Waltz said. "You could see the air moving" as the bullets rushed past. The bullets looked like "bright yellow lasers, flying up and down, in front of me, behind me, over me."

Waltz saw of one of the weapons shooting at him—"there was a massive flame belching at me from the end of the gun"— and recognized it to be a PKM, one of the insurgents' main weapons. The gun's short bipod legs hung over the wadi's wall, only thirty yards to Waltz's front left. Worse, the insurgent was elevated about ten feet, shooting down on Waltz's team. The gun was raking up and down the patrol, "trying to get as many of us as he could." The situation was grim. "He had us dead to rights."

After that initial burst of fire, Waltz saw Sergeant Major Sumar lying on the ground where he had first fallen. The interpreter, who had been standing next to Waltz, dropped in a whimpering heap at Waltz's feet.

Waltz was totally exposed, with no trees or bushes nearby. There was a small wall that stood three or four feet high to his right, and Waltz believed "90 percent of the rest of the Army would have dived for cover" behind that wall because that was the logical thing to do. Or they would have at least gotten down to the ground, to make themselves smaller targets. But Waltz reflexively relied on his training and did the opposite.

His training before deployment had emphasized clearing urban structures, which taught him to stand straight up with his shoulders square toward the shooter. "That is where you have most of your armor," Waltz explained. So he took a step to his left to untangle his feet from the sobbing interpreter and squared his shoulders. He raised his M4 rifle and started firing. He couldn't see what he was shooting at, as it wasn't quite dark enough for his night-vision goggles to make out the targets. "I was just shooting at the muzzle flashes."

After firing several rounds, Waltz felt the bolt of the rifle slam forward . . . and nothing happened. He canted the rifle around to his left so he could see the bolt. Two rounds had jammed together in the chamber. "It was a classic double feed," Waltz remembered. So the rifle was inoperable. "That," Waltz later recalled, "is when time slowed down."

Waltz swept the jammed rifle to his left while simultaneously bringing up his pistol with his right hand. It was a fluid motion that Waltz's sergeants had made him practice countless times in training.

As he switched his weapon, another burst of fire raked up and down the wadi. This time, the bright yellow lasers popped past his left ear. "It was so damn loud," Waltz recalled with a wince. The shots were not wild. He doesn't know how he avoided getting hit. "It was a *Pulp Fiction* moment," he said, referring to the movie's scene in which a volley of close-range shots missed their target, marking the wall behind the character with an ominous silhouette. By this time, Waltz noticed that there was more than one gun shooting at them—maybe even three different shooters, all at point-blank range.

But Waltz didn't flinch. He withstood the enemy's machine-gun fire, standing in the middle of the wadi and shooting back with a pistol. He had no cover, no grenades, and no helmet.

"I thought for sure Mike was going to get killed," Brian recalled. He took great pains to convey just how close Waltz and the insurgents were. "It was an incredibly short distance," he said, adding that from his vantage point, "their muzzle flashes were nearly touching." Brian described with admiration how everyone was scrambling for "nonexistent cover," but Waltz remained standing out in the open, using a pistol to take on two shooters with machine guns who were hiding behind a thick wall at night. "Mike knows he is lucky to be alive."

Waltz believed his training got him through those harrowing moments. He had never been in combat before, and he readily conceded that he didn't know how he would perform under duress. "All my life I had thought about combat," he said, "and you never know what you'll react like. In that instant, are you going to get petrified? Are you going to panic?" Being a leader only heightened the pressure: "How are you going to react? How will you perform personally? How will you perform in front of your men? Certainly all of those things are weighing on your mind."

Waltz believed that it is impossible to know how an individual will react under those circumstances. While a person's response to duress is somewhat innate, he believed training could greatly affect the reaction. "It minimizes the likelihood that you'll panic," he said. "In [the] military, you train, train, train. It's like going to ten years of football practice, but never playing a game." The ambush in the wadi was "a serious baptism," Waltz said, and moments like that are "why you do the drills."

His training helped him avoid getting panicked and cut through a wave of emotions. At first, when he realized they were being attacked, Waltz was livid. "From an emotional standpoint, I just became so frickin' angry, and I just started unloading." That continued through the switch to the pistol: "I emptied my entire magazine."

His anger, however, eventually gave way to fear. When he'd emptied the pistol's magazine of fifteen rounds, the top of gun locked backwards, awaiting a new clip. Just as the pistol locked, a PKM burst rang out next to his head. At that moment, with his second gun empty and the enemy shots zeroing in on his head,

"I went from angry to petrified." The desperation of his situation came crashing down on him, and he asked himself: "What the fuck are you doing standing in the middle of a wadi face-to-face with a machine gun with a pistol?! I'm fucking dead," he thought. "There is no way I'm going to match the machine gun."

Despite his fear, Waltz stayed focused. He remembered the short stone wall that—"by the grace of God"—lay to his right. The wall that he'd dismissed just a few moments earlier was now a heaven-sent gift. It wouldn't give him much cover, but it was certainly better than nothing.

He stumbled lustily toward the wall, stepping over the interpreter at his feet and flopping over the wall. Weighed down with gear, his dive was hardly graceful. He landed with a heavy thud and rolled onto his back, kicking dust up in the air and throwing night-vision equipment all over his face.

He changed out the magazine in the pistol as insurgent rounds pinged around him. Lying on his back, with his feet toward the insurgents, Waltz held the pistol in his outstretched arms and aimed between his legs. He still couldn't see specific targets, other than the horrifying flames projecting from enemies' rifles. So he aimed at the muzzle flashes and fired away. His goal was simple: "Keep volume of fire on the enemy." He hoped that his shots, even if inaccurate, would force the insurgents to keep their heads down and slow the volume of fire against his team. Maybe—if Waltz got lucky—he would hit one of them.

The situation was dire. The insurgents were basically shooting fish in a barrel, and Waltz was the closest fish. He had already seen one of his team get hit and had no idea whether anyone behind him was still alive. He believed he was going to die and was simply hoping to stave off the inevitable for a few precious moments.

And then things got worse.

As he lay behind the short wall and feebly battled at least three enemy machine guns and rifles with his pistol, Waltz didn't think things could deteriorate much further. Then he saw new tracer rounds enter the fray. But not from the insurgents' position—they were coming from behind him. Waves of bullets clipped the trees above him, and grenades flew overhead and exploded nearby.

Waltz quickly recognized that the tracers were from the powerful fifty-caliber machine guns that coalition forces used. With that, a sickening feeling enveloped Waltz: the new rounds were friendly fire from the backup units parked at the police station on the edge of town. The activity of the ambush had evidently drawn them in, and, despite the no-fire orders, they were unleashing a devastating assault of grenades and fifty-caliber fire. "They were just lighting up the village," Waltz said, "and us." Brian used slightly more colorful imagery: "Our position looked like the stage of a Pink Floyd laser light show."

Waltz fumed at the backup units. He had specifically instructed them that the village was a no-fire zone—they were not supposed to fire in the direction of the patrol, even if they observed combat activity. "Instead of a no-fire zone," Waltz lamented, "it was everybody shooting." Worse, Waltz recalled, the backup forces did not have any night-vision equipment, which might have enabled them to distinguish between friend and foe. So they were essentially shooting blindly into the village.

That's when it dawned on him—between the insurgent fire immediately in front of him and the coalition fire raining down on the village from behind, his team was now caught in a cross fire. The desperation of that moment was evident on Waltz's face years later. "I thought we were gonna die. I really did. I thought we were in a *bad* way."

Waltz kept shooting, aiming between his legs and unloading his pistol's second magazine toward the far side of the wadi. He wanted to keep pressure on the shooters and change the situation quickly, so he instinctively reached for a grenade. But he'd opted for a light load and had left his grenades behind. He cursed himself under his breath and kept pinging away with his pistol.

The team's communications sergeant scurried up next to him, having run up the wadi directly into the enemy fire and plopped roughly over the short wall. Waltz yelled at the sergeant to throw a grenade. The sergeant whipped one out of a pocket promptly, but throwing the device wasn't so smooth. Long before this mission, they had put in an extra security measure to ensure that the grenade wouldn't go off unexpectedly: wrapping thick tape over the safety clip and the pin. "I'll never forget it," Waltz recalled, as he scrunched his face anxiously. "[The sergeant] pulled it out and was fucking with the tape. I cussed at him while I'm still firing through the magazine with my pistol."

The sergeant finally ripped off the tape and tossed the grenade over the wall. Waltz heard the explosive detonate. Then he heard screeching and groaning from the other side of the wall. The insurgents' rifles then fell quiet.

Waltz had emptied his second pistol magazine by this point, so he took the opportunity to put in a new one—his last fifteen rounds. Brian then shouted over to them, beckoning them to join him in a small thatch of trees sitting a bit farther down the wadi. Waltz knew he had to move to better cover and scrambled with his sergeant over to the medic's position.

As Waltz stumbled into the thicket of trees, he realized that he had dropped his night-vision gear in the wadi. "That was really bad," Brian recalled. The ability to see at night was a massive advantage for US troops and "we feared the [night-vision gear] would end up in enemy hands." But retrieving the equipment would mean going directly back into the kill zone. Waltz didn't fret about it for too long, Brian said, borrowing his night-vision goggles and darting back into the wadi. Brian provided cover from the grove of trees as Waltz quickly grabbed the equipment and hustled back to the medic's position.

Hiding amongst the trees, Waltz tried to assess their situation. He heard some movement from the other side of wall, but couldn't tell what was happening. He didn't know whether the insurgents—if they'd survived the grenade explosion—were maneuvering to a new location to continue the assault, or whether enemy reinforcements were preparing for stage two of the ambush. He called out to the interpreter to get more information, but the man remained curled up on the wadi floor, sobbing and barely responding to Waltz's voice.

More pressingly, Waltz knew Sergeant Major Sumar had gotten hit and lay helpless just thirty feet away. Waltz thought he could save the man's life, and his conscience wouldn't let him sit back and do nothing—even if that meant running right back into the middle of the kill zone for the second time.

Waltz called out to Brian that he was going back to save the wounded Afghan and told the medic to prepare to treat a casualty. The medic suggested that they should wait until the other patrol team joined them, so they would have extra cover fire in case of a second assault. But there was no doubt in Waltz's mind. He had to go back and get Sumar now. Waltz did not want to lose the opportunity to save the Afghan if he was alive. And, even if the sergeant major was already dead, Waltz wanted to deny the enemy his weapon and equipment.

Waltz then told his sergeant to provide cover. "I didn't know if I was going to run down there and get hosed." With the sergeant unloading his rifle toward the opposite wall, Waltz ducked underneath the cover fire and scurried out of the thatch of trees. Exposed in the wadi once again, he sprinted toward the wounded man.

Waltz didn't know whether the insurgents were shooting at him as he ran up the riverbed—the only thought in his mind was saving Sumar. He ran over to where the Afghan was lying and lunged forward to grab him. He touched Sumar's torso—the man's uniform was soaking wet. Waltz wasn't certain whether he was still alive, although he thought he heard faint gasps.

Waltz grabbed Sumar's wet gear and yanked him down the wadi toward the other Americans. The cheap, thin fabric of the Afghan's gear ripped off in Waltz's hands. He chucked the shreds to the side and reached out again. This time, he got a firm grasp and carried the man down the wadi. It was not the heroic extraction of a Hollywood disaster movie: "I ended up manhandling him back and dragging him out of the kill zone as [the other Americans] fired over my head." Waltz could hear Sumar gasping in his arms. The man's blood covered Waltz's hands and drenched his uniform.

After what felt like an eternity exposed in the deep wadi, Waltz finally hauled the man to the grove where the other coalition soldiers waited. But by that time, Waltz knew, Sumar was dead. "He literally died in my arms as I was carrying him out."

When Waltz arrived back at the grove in the wadi, the situation had deteriorated rapidly. "It was pandemonium," Waltz recalled. Sumar was the Afghan unit's first casualty, and the remaining Afghans were in disarray, arguing with each other about how to get out of the wadi and what to do with the man's body. Waltz tried to assert control by organizing the team into a rough perimeter—basically a circle in which they faced outward so that they could watch for enemy activity without shooting each other.

Those were terrifying moments, Brian recalled. The shooting had stopped, but they all understood that could change at any moment. The medic later wrote to his family: "From my position on the . . . perimeter, I could hear, but not quite see, more movement in the orchard. It then occurred to me that the entire village may be mobilized against us. I figured there must have been about a thousand fighting-aged males, 12–50 years old, who lived in the vicinity. We wouldn't have had any chance if they pinpointed us."

Waltz radioed back to the police station to tell the backup unit about the contact. He tried to turn on his GPS, but the batteries were dead. He cursed himself again—he habitually put new batteries in his equipment for every mission, but he just plain forgot before this patrol. "I know better," Waltz said shamefully. "I had done that a hundred times before, and the one time you get complacent, it kills you."

He pulled the batteries out of his flashlight and threw them gruffly into the GPS. Then he restarted the machine and waited for it to reboot. It was a surreal moment, waiting for a computer to start up in the middle of a firefight.

Waltz eventually got the GPS working, but the team's focus had wavered again. It was back to panicked chaos. Waltz appeared to be losing control of the Afghans, as they were openly discussing leaving the Americans behind with the sergeant major's body while making their own way out of the town. The Afghans refused to touch Sumar's body, which infuriated Waltz. Worse, the interpreter was still an inconsolable mess; Waltz had to snap the man back to his senses by literally shaking him by the lapels. To top it off, Waltz had lost radio contact with the backup units at the police station. At the same time, he knew his men in the other dismounted patrol were making their way through the village toward his position, and he was petrified the shaken Afghans with no night vision would hear them approaching and open fire. The situation was unraveling quickly.

After several fits and starts at reasserting some control, Waltz finally lost his temper. In a Hollywood moment, Waltz pulled out his pistol and fired two shots straight up in the air. Everyone snapped to. "The Afghans immediately got to the ground," Brian recalled, "thinking we were again being attacked." In the lull that followed, Waltz insisted that the Afghans carry their comrade back to the police station, saying to the team through the sobbing interpreter: "Someone else is going to die if you don't start moving that body right now."

Brian described the rest of Waltz's impromptu speech, observing that he remained calm and controlled throughout: "Mike explained in a normal voice [that] everyone was staying with him. And if they wanted to die right there, that was fine with him; otherwise they had to pick up that body and move out." The medic notes that he and other Americans in the team were willing to carry Sumar's body, "but we backed Mike in one of those much-needed, all-or-nothing, 'We're-burning-our-boats-behind-us' examples of effective leadership."

Waltz's stern words seemed to knock some sense into the team. The men grabbed a ladder from a nearby yard for a make-shift stretcher, loaded Sumar's body on top, and started down the wadi toward their base. It was a grueling hike through the darkened maze of deep-walled wadis and goat trails, all while carrying the ladder with a lifeless two-hundred-pound body. It reminded Waltz of those Special Forces training exercises, except this time they weren't carrying bags of sand.

Their progress was "agonizingly slow," Brian recalled. Throughout the trek back to their base, they expected to be ambushed again. "Every corner, rooftop, door, window, wall, and tree was treated as if it concealed a potential threat." To make matters worse, the Afghans didn't have night-vision equipment, so the medic later joked, "when they weren't bumping into one another with their assault rifles, they looked like Jodie Foster feeling around in the dark as in the penultimate scene of *Silence of the Lambs*."

It would be two hours before the demoralized, exhausted team arrived at the police station. The coalition unit with their heavy machine guns back at the base never offered to help. The team later learned from one of the coalition's embarrassed snipers that he had been observing in his thermal night-vision scope up to fifty insurgents in three different groups trying to find the trapped team, but his officer in charge ignored his pleas to go help the Americans and Afghans down in the village.

The next morning, as Sumar's body was being loaded onto a truck to go to his home outside Jalalabad, Waltz and his team took up a collection of money for the man's family. An older Afghan interpreter—a different one from the blubbering mess from the night before—was also from Jalalabad and was going back there a couple of weeks later. He volunteered to take the donations to the sergeant major's family. All of the Americans contributed, with a couple of other coalition troops kicking in some additional money. All told, they gathered around five hundred to six hundred dollars in Afghanis, the local currency. It was the equivalent of the sergeant major's salary for five or six months.

Weeks later, the interpreter returned from Jalalabad. He described to Waltz and his teammates how distraught Sumar's wife and family were about his death. He said the whole village was distraught—it turns out that he was a leader not only in his military unit, but in his familial clan as well. The interpreter also brought troubling news about the family's future prospects. Per Afghan custom, the options for the family were not terribly attractive. They could be separated and dispersed among various family members, and Sumar's widow would likely get married off to a family member, possibly one of the sergeant major's brothers. Even worse, the interpreter said, at least two of Sumar's boys would probably be forced go to a madrassa.

Hearing those words changed Waltz. He instantly had a new mission: "I wanted to do everything I could to avoid that." He thought back to the towering figure he had grown to respect and the conversation on the hike outside Kora. He could not sit idly by as Sumar's nightmare—that his boys would go to madrassas—came true. So Waltz dedicated himself to provide for Sumar's family—to at least match the man's salary—to keep his boys from going to a madrassa.

Every few weeks for the rest of his deployment—which lasted five more months—Waltz salted away a month's salary for Sumar's family. As with the initial collection when the sergeant major died, the older interpreter from Jalalabad faithfully carried Waltz's gift to the family on his visits home.

When Waltz's tour ended in September 2006, however, he returned to the United States and had no way to send the family any money. So he set out to orchestrate a mechanism to transfer those funds to the family in a safe and reliable manner. That was no easy feat, Waltz said, as Afghanistan has little of a modern banking system and no mail whatsoever. Waltz struggled for months to make it work. As time wore on, he grew increasingly frustrated, because he feared what was happening to Sumar's family without his support.

Waltz eventually used a contact in Kabul to establish a relationship with a trustworthy bank. He recognized that the bank was the linchpin for the entire idea and scrutinized the organization carefully. "I went through an enormous effort to do as much vetting as possible," Waltz said. He understood that Afghan bankers often took bribes to allow unauthorized access to accounts or, in the case of a poor widow, could simply steal funds for themselves. He was also worried the men in her village would take the money. Once he was comfortable that the bank had legitimate safeguards and a branch in Jalalabad that Sumar's widow could visit in person, as well as a particular bank manager that could be trusted, he moved forward.

He worked with the manager to establish a process for him to wire money to an account established for Sumar's family. Over countless e-mails and phone calls, they identified potential pitfalls and vulnerabilities that could create problems, and Waltz decided to put certain limits on the account: only Sumar's widow would be authorized to withdraw money from the account, and she would be limited to withdrawing her husband's monthly salary. Those restrictions, Waltz explained, were for her benefit as much as his. With these limits in place, she would have some control over her future, and the men in the village wouldn't be able to force her to go to the bank and empty the account.

It took almost a full year to make it happen. But once in place, the process worked well: Waltz wired money from Washington, and she visited the bank in Jalalabad every month to withdraw the specified sum. Waltz also communicated with the bank manager periodically to make sure the transactions were working as intended. Waltz continued to send her money for the ensuing five years and has no plans to stop.

Sumar's widow has never known who is sending the money—the interpreter told her just that it came from a "friendly American" who was with her husband when he died. That's just the way Waltz wants it to be.

Waltz, as well as the American sergeant who fought with him, received a Bronze Star Medal with a V for valor for their actions during the firefight in the wadi. Waltz would receive another Bronze Star Medal with Valor for his actions during a second ambush during the 2006 deployment. Brian, the senior medic who was in the wadi with them that night, nominated Waltz and the other sergeant for the awards. The fact that an enlisted man in his team—rather than a superior officer—nominated him for the honors had special meaning for Waltz. Likewise, Brian said that nominating Waltz for the medals was "one of my proudest moments as a soldier."

Following his return from that deployment, Waltz continued his work at the Pentagon and later served in the White House as special assistant to the vice president for South Asia and counterterrorism. In that capacity, Waltz was the principal advisor to Vice President Dick Cheney on Afghan affairs. He drew on his experiences throughout his Afghanistan deployments, including the firefight in Kora, in formulating policy for the Afghan conflict. He was in the perfect position to try to help bridge any disconnect between the intent of strategic policy decisions and how they were being executed on the ground. He developed a productive relationship with the vice president's national security team, who respected him for his on-the-ground experience with the rural Afghan tribes. With Waltz, they came as close as they could to a warrior-scholar. Based on his experiences in-country, Waltz advocated for addressing such issues as the complicated command-and-control structure in place,

NATO's failings, and Americans' lack of knowledge about the Afghan tribes.

After his time at the White House, Waltz returned to Afghanistan for a third deployment in 2009. During this tour, he was charged with multiple Special Forces teams along four provinces on the Pakistani border. While he was in-country, Waltz couldn't pass up the opportunity to check on Sumar's family. He asked one of his Afghan interpreters to visit Sumar's widow in Jalalabad. The man did so and returned with information for Waltz. During the lull in Waltz's payments—when he was developing the system to send her money following his return to the United States in 2006—Sumar's widow had been forced to send two of her boys to a madrassa. Waltz was crushed when he heard that, but his spirits soared when he learned her sons returned to the family as soon as Waltz's payments restarted. His donations to the family were literally the only thing keeping those boys from the madrassa. The interpreter also had pictures—after years of sending the family money, it was the first time Waltz actually saw what they looked like. "The kids are beautiful," he said, beaming with a wonderful grin. "They're gorgeous." Waltz, of course, viewed his relationship with that Afghan family as a microcosm of the larger war: "We are going to win this war one family at a time."

Stephen Sanford in Mosul, Iraq, in 2005. Courtesy of
Stephen Sanford.

Steve Sanford
"The Worst Soldier in the History of the Army"

"**I** was the worst soldier in the history of the Army," Steve Sanford said with a mischievous smirk. He described his gaffes and wisecracks with an impish pride. Once, Sanford recalled, with that puckish grin spreading across his face, his sergeant instructed him to get a haircut—and Sanford insisted on consulting with his union representative first to file a grievance. The result? "Lots of push-ups."

In fact, Steve Sanford spent a significant chunk of his Army service in the push-up position. He just could not get the hang of the Army Way, as he calls it. Packing his gear incorrectly, wearing the wrong boots for lawn mowing, whatever—Sanford always seemed to screw it up. He demonstrated his superiors' typical response with a simple pantomime: dismissively pointing to the ground, silently ordering more push-ups. His penchant for wisecracks and back talk just added fuel to the fire. He was once chastised for wearing the wrong socks with his combat boots—he wore a white pair, not the required green ones. "Who cares what color socks I'm wearing?!" he asked incredulously. "They're covered up!" That, he said, was a no-no. More push-ups.

Sanford was quick to clarify that he wasn't really a bad soldier—he was just a bad soldier *when on base*. "There are garrison soldiers, and there are combat soldiers," he said. "Some people are both. I'm not." All he cared about was performing well in combat. Sanford described a scene in Clint Eastwood's movie *Heartbreak Ridge* in which a career desk jockey mocks Eastwood's character, saying that the hardened gunnery sergeant should be caged like an animal with a sign "Break Glass in Case of War." That was exactly how Sanford viewed himself. So he didn't care one whit about sweeping gravel and packing gear in a specified manner. "If you need your lawn mowed by 5:00, I'm not your guy; but if there's an emergency situation—somebody is bleeding, or there's a fire, or there's a shooting—I'm the guy to have around."

Sanford would have the opportunity to prove that during a bloody firefight in Mosul, Iraq, in November 2005.

At a very young age, Steve Sanford became fascinated by all things military—history, guns, fighter planes, tanks, you name it. While other kids might be reading the Hardy Boys or Nancy Drew, young Steve would be in the local bookstore memorizing page numbers of key planes in *Jane's Encyclopedia of Aircraft*. One of the first books he read was Chuck Yeager's autobiography, and a reverential look came over his eyes years later when talking about the World War II double ace who went on to be the first man to break the sound barrier.

While the kids in his rural Michigan town might play kick the can, Steve and his friends would scurry around town conducting war games. He recalled pretending to be frog men with his buddies and making fake bombs out of Play-Doh. They would sneak into the marina at the nearby lake with their wetsuits and snorkel under the boats to stick the Play-Doh "explosives" on unsuspecting hulls. "Some of the stuff," he said with a chuckle, "would probably be considered deviant terrorist behavior." Now, Sanford said, those things would likely get a kid a long visit from the FBI.

Sanford guessed that he became so enthralled with the military world because of his three older brothers. He idolized them, and all three were in the Army when he was an impressionable young kid. There was another relationship that fueled Sanford's military fascination: in his late teens, while he was taking classes at a local college, Sanford heard a speech by Joe Beyrle, a World War II hero that lived in his hometown of Muskegon, Michigan. Sanford thought Beyrle's speech was captivating and weaseled his way into meeting the elderly hero. That spawned a friendship. It was an odd pairing, with Sanford the teenager having dinner at the older man's house to discuss war stories, but it worked. "With my interest in military history and Beyrle *being* military history, Joe was someone I wanted to talk to," Sanford said. He had pored over historical accounts of D-day, but "knowing that there were people who were running through the hedgerows trying to evade the Germans is different from talking to someone who was running through the hedgerows trying to evade the Germans."

All of these military influences, particularly Beyrle and Yeager, had a profound impact on the young man. He marveled at Beyrle's story of survival and dedication. The man parachuted into France before D-day and was later captured by the Germans, nearly starving to death at a POW camp. Sanford was awestruck at how he wouldn't give up: "He didn't just go home and have a beer." To the contrary, Beyrle escaped and continued fighting against the Nazis . . . with the Russian Army. Sanford likewise admired Yeager, who was shot down on his third mission, evaded capture, worked with the French resistance, and, when he was returned to his squadron in England, insisted on flying once again. The man would go on to become a legendary pilot, shooting down more than a dozen German planes. These heroes set a high bar in his mind: they were "people who did what they were supposed to do and wouldn't quit—they just kept going and going." Sanford knew that it was a standard he had to meet.

After he graduated from high school, Sanford took classes at a local college, not surprisingly focusing on history, with a fair number of political science and government classes. He also became an emergency medical technician, completing clinical rotations and studying IVs, EKGs, and a host of other trauma-related topics. He later worked for armed security contractors around the world, including in the Middle East. Although he was never personally targeted, he was uncomfortably close to a few rocket-propelled grenades and other unsavory ballistics and was shot once when a bullet ricocheted off nearby pavement and skimmed his calf.

When he returned to the United States, something had started to bother him. The US military at that time was engaged in a bloody battle for the insurgent-infested city of Fallujah, Iraq. Sanford watched the news of the battle, and his conscience started urging him to join the military. The country was at war and needed help. "If you live in a country, you have a responsibility to defend it or answer when they need you," he said. "It was my personal belief that everyone owes something that cannot be paid by taxes. Something that you have to do, whether it's volunteering at the local fire department, being a lifeguard, helping out with schoolkids, or going in the military, Coast Guard, or search and rescue. I think it's important to be able to say that you've done something to help your community. I think people owe that to the country and everyone else."

At twenty-four, he would be a bit older than a typical enlistee, but he believed his previous experiences as an armed security contractor and an EMT had prepared him well for military service. "I knew my way around a rifle," he said. He was also moved by the knowledge that when he deployed some nineteen-year-old kid could return home.

Sanford remembers the moment that sealed the deal in his mind. He saw an image of a Marine wounded during a Fallujah firefight. "I remember seeing this picture of a Marine—he couldn't have been eighteen—he didn't shave yet," Sanford recalled, with mounting intensity in his voice. "He was all bloody. I remember thinking: 'A year ago, this kid probably didn't know one end of the rifle from another. It's probably the first time he's been out of the country. His most recent big deal was his *prom*. Now he's in *Fallujah.*' And then I thought: 'What am I doing, sitting here?!'"

So he enlisted a couple of weeks later. He employed a unique process of elimination to figure out which service to join. His main goal was to get action early and often, and that largely drove his decision. The Navy was too far removed from combat for his taste. "The days of 'wooden ships and iron men' are long gone. We don't put together boarding parties with cutlasses and lash the ships together anymore. So the Navy was out." The Air Force suffered a similar fate. He had long joked that the Air Force was simply "The Department of Defense Flying Club," although he concedes that he would have liked to be a pilot. But his six foot three frame and his substandard eyesight eliminated that possibility, and with that the Air Force as well.

That left the Marine Corps and the Army, both of which were highly attractive to Sanford. He ultimately chose the Army over the Marines because his whole family had been in the Army, and he knew no one in the Navy or Marines. The Army also gave him a better deal, agreeing in the enlistment contract that he would have an early opportunity to compete for a slot in the Special Forces. So that sealed the deal, and in January 2005, Sanford enlisted in the US Army.

A few weeks later, in early 2005, he started basic training. While many soldiers break out in hives at the mere mention of boot camp, Sanford thrived in that environment. He loved learning about combat tactics and pushing himself both physically and mentally. He described the drill instructors as very knowledgeable and just plain "awesome." Boot camp, Sanford said, was "the second-most fun I've ever had in my life"—second only to his deployment to Iraq. He quickly catches himself and adds, with his voice trailing off: "I suppose I should say becoming a father . . ."

One moment from boot camp sticks out in Sanford's mind. On the day that Sanford and his class graduated from basic training, the sergeant in charge of Sanford's forty-man platoon told his men that he read the *Army Times* every week for the list of casualties. He said that none of his men had ever been on that list, and he wanted it to stay that way. Months later, however, after that class deployed to Iraq, names from that platoon would start appearing in the *Army Times*.

Following graduation from boot camp in the spring of 2005, Sanford was assigned to the 172nd Stryker Brigade Combat Team (SBCT) stationed at Fort Wainwright, Alaska. It was exactly what Sanford wanted—an infantry platoon with a fast-approaching deployment, right in the middle of the action. Roughly forty of the 120 men in his basic training company were also stationed there, so the deep relationships Sanford had formed in basic training would develop even further in the months on base and, later, in Iraq. "At that point," Sanford said with a chuckle, "I'd lived with a little Korean guy named Moon longer than my wife."

Fort Wainwright was a tough time for Sanford. This was when he was "the worst soldier in the history of the Army" and spent much of his time in push-up position. He was stuck on a base, mowing lawns and sweeping gravel, when there was a war going on. He understood that they would be deployed to Iraq in a matter of months, but he just couldn't wait. "I'm not good with idle hands," he said sheepishly. Sanford comforted himself with the belief that famed war heroes like Sergeant York of World War I and Audie Murphy of World War II were not good garrison soldiers either. "They got in a lot of trouble too," he said with smile.

Sanford was quick to note that he was mischievous only about menial chores and the Army's seemingly endless list of rules that weren't related to combat; when it came time to train, however, Sanford was an eager student, volunteering for every available practice session at the firing range and begging for all sorts of weapons training. He became proficient in a wide range of weapons, becoming qualified to use several types of guns, even ones he would never realistically use. "If they would let me shoot it," Sanford recalled, "I would head down to the range and qualify for it."

After Sanford spent the spring and most of the summer at Fort Wainwright, it was time to deploy. On August 15, 2005, Sanford and his SBCT deployed to Mosul, Iraq. The city was a cauldron of hostility at the time. Beyond the overt guerrilla fighting between US troops and al-Qaeda affiliates and other insurgent groups, there were simmering conflicts between the city's various ethnic groups—Shiites, Sunnis, Christians, and Kurds. "So while a bomb may not have been planted for us," Sanford said, "we still got it."

Sanford's unit had two primary responsibilities: patrols through the city and cordon-and-search missions. On patrols, Sanford's platoon of forty men would split up into their eight-wheeled armored fighting vehicles, called Strykers. Ten men would fit in each Stryker: a driver, a vehicle commander, and eight infantry. Whenever a Stryker was running, five of the men in the vehicle had to be alert and "on the guns," as Sanford said. The squad leader would be standing up in the hatch outside of the armor, and two infantry men would stand "air guard," which meant they stood out of two hatches in the back of the vehicle to watch its entire perimeter. When the squad dismounted from the Stryker (such as when they arrived at their destination and were preparing to raid a house), the driver, vehicle commander, and one air guard would stay back with the vehicle, while the other seven went on the raid.

The cordon-and-search missions were designed to lock down an area of the city and capture any weapons caches or bomb-making materials. Sanford's unit would cordon off a few blocks in the city and search every single building in the secured area. On slow days, they would search three to four houses; other days were much busier, with the unit sweeping through five to ten houses in an hour. Every house, it seemed, had a weapon, and some had grenades and booby traps, which slowed them down considerably.

The residents were generally pleasant and understanding, Sanford recalled. "They knew we were there to root out al-Qaeda. They didn't want them there as much as we didn't." On a typical sweep, Sanford remembered, the Americans would knock on the door and ask whether the residents needed anything. Many residents invited them in for tea, and the Americans would jump at the chance to foster positive relations with the Iraqis, sitting on the couch, removing their helmets (but not their vests), and sipping tea with the family. They would enjoy small talk about the weather or sports and try to address the Iraqis' problems, like inconsistent power supply, plumbing issues, or sewage disposal. "We would fix what we could," Sanford said. He recalled helping some Iraqis repair a broken sewage line—"I smelled very bad after that day." Other times the troops would just visit with the locals. They would crack off-color jokes with the men ("rude man-jokes") and give the family food.

Sanford's favorite interactions with the Iraqis were with the kids. His unit would occasionally stop on a patrol and hand out all sorts of toys to Iraqi children—books, coloring books, footballs, soccer balls, trucks, all donated by Americans back home. The neighborhood kids would crowd around the men, trying to get their attention with frantic calls of "Mister! Mister! Mister!" So the men called them "Mister Monsters." Sanford recalled that the Mister Monsters went ballistic for candy, so they would hand out bags and bags of candy all over Mosul. With all the candy they gave away, Sanford said, "Iraq is going to have a huge dental problem."

Sanford's first three months in Iraq were busy, but relatively quiet. His unit had been on an eight-hour patrol schedule, meaning they would patrol for eight hours and then have eight hours off. So he was constantly going out on missions and patrols, but that did not bother him one bit. "That's why I went there." The unit had several minor skirmishes here and there, but nothing significant. He spent more time fighting off Mister Monsters than insurgents.

That would all change in the early morning hours on November 19, 2005.

Around 4:00 that morning, Sanford's entire platoon was roused for a patrol. As they grumpily loaded the four Strykers in the predawn hours, the men complained about how stupid it was to go out on patrol so early in the morning. They eventually started playing "grab-ass," as Sanford described it, quickly turning their sights on one of the guys, a younger guy named Christopher Alcozer.

"We were pals," Sanford said, describing Chris as a "young, full-of-life kind of guy." They had gone through boot camp together and were now in the same squad. Over time, Sanford said, he had grown protective of his friend. Their environment—an Army infantry platoon awaiting deployment to a war zone—was rough and tumble. "It was like a college fraternity," Sanford said, "but with guns." Boisterous ribbing and getting in trouble were the norm. But Chris was "more of a gentle type," Sanford said, recalling that he had majored in music in college. So he looked out for Chris, like an older brother watching over a younger sibling on the playground. They would hang out and occasionally raise some Cain. "We did some juvenile things together," Sanford said, declining to provide specifics.

But Sanford could not protect Chris from the ribbing that morning. Chris had just returned from leave, where he had just become engaged to his girlfriend. That, of course, created wonderful fodder for his unforgiving mates. In fact Sanford couldn't help himself and joined in the merciless teasing. "We were giving him a raft of shit," Sanford recalled, flashing the mischievous smirk again.

Eventually, Chris was granted a reprieve when the platoon departed on the patrol. As they weaved through the city's streets, the men sat in the Strykers, tired and bored out of their mind, grumpily rehashing the stupidity of a 4:00 a.m. patrol. After driving around for roughly an hour and a half, the platoon received a call from Iraqi police requesting help with a raid on a nearby house.

The platoon promptly drove to the house and cordoned off the area. Sanford's Stryker sat about one hundred yards down the street, primarily responsible for guarding the perimeter and blocking anyone from entering or leaving the area, rather than providing gunfire in support of the raiding team. Sanford was standing in a hatch as one of the two air guards. It was dark and there were few working streetlights. As he scanned his eyes over the street, checking out neighboring houses and the darkened alleys lying in between, Sanford listened to the raiding party on the vehicle's intercom system, which was piped in through the headphones in his helmet.

That's when he heard the first blast—a concussive boom coming from his headphones. Then came shouting—it was the raiding teams: "Oh shit! Medic! We've been hit!" Two more explosions followed, along with faint echoes of machine-gun fire. Sanford recognized the sound of the explosions—they were mortar shells. Sanford learned later that the insurgents had replaced the triggering mechanism with the fuse of a hand grenade. They were essentially lobbing oversized grenades at the raiding teams as they entered the house. "'Bowling for Americans' is I guess what you'd call it," Sanford said.

Sitting one hundred yards away, the other guys in Sanford's Stryker had not heard the explosions or the raiders' call for help. Sanford heard them only because he was wearing a helmet with intercom headphones. As soon as he heard the explosions, Sanford became a one-man flurry of activity. In a not-so-fluid motion, he ducked out of the hatch, hit the button to lower the vehicle's back ramp, ripped off the intercom helmet, and put on his regular Kevlar helmet, all while yelling that the other squads needed backup.

The rest of the men in the back of the Stryker had no idea what was going on. Sanford again hollered that the raiding team had gotten hit. He sprinted down the ramp before it had even hit the ground. The rest of the guys hurried out of the vehicle behind him. They raced down the street and crouched in front of the front gate to the property. "It took the rest of the squad a little longer because they had been napping because of the hour and we thought it was another bullshit raid."

Sanford and his teammates, along with an assortment of other guys who were securing the other perimeter, peered into the property from the gate. The target was a typical Iraqi house—two stories, with nondescript brown walls made of cinderblock or plaster. There was a small, grassy courtyard stretching about ten to fifteen feet in front of the house. As with most Iraqi houses, a dense wall standing about eight feet tall surrounded the property.

A group of six men gathered to storm the house. There was no real selection process. It was akin to grade schoolers picking teams for a sandlot kickball game. Sanford was in the group. As they ran past the gate and through the courtyard, one of the Americans from the initial raiding party stumbled out of the house, bleeding profusely from his arm, with his weapon dangling at his side. He told them that the rest of the Americans from the initial raid were trapped inside the house.

Sanford jumped up on the front step and leaned the left side of his body against the house's front wall. Using the doorframe for cover, Sanford turned his head around the doorjamb and peeked inside the house. He couldn't see much of anything. It was just too dark. He could see the "nasty-ass linoleum from the seventies" on the floor, which was covered in fresh blood.

The six men regrouped at the front door, lined up with two sergeants leading the group, and pushed into the house. Sanford was fourth in the line.

As they entered the house, they spotted the American casualties in the kitchen off to the left. The two sergeants in the front of the line and the two guys behind darted off to help them. That left Sanford and one other soldier alone as they moved farther down the unlit hallway stretching out in front of them. "All of a sudden, it went from six guys to just the two of us," Sanford recalled.

A room sat at the end of the hall, off to the right. The two men tore down the hall, with the other man in the lead. As he turned into the room, a barrage of fire erupted from inside. The man was hit immediately in the upper arm and said to Sanford: "I think I got shot." But he didn't move out of the way and remained standing in front of the doorway as rounds shot from inside the room pinged all around. Sanford yelled at him to move, which seemed to knock sense into him, and he promptly ran down the hall and out of the house.

Sanford then prepared to turn the corner—where his teammate had just received a volley of fire—and enter the room. "Somebody's gotta kill the guy," Sanford explained. "He's not going to stop shooting at my guys until he runs out of bullets or I kill him." So Sanford hopped into the doorway.

As soon as he turned the corner, he knew he was in trouble. The room was about ten feet by fifteen feet, with a couch sitting perpendicular to the door and a large chair facing the couch. Sanford believes there were two shooters, one behind the chair and one behind the couch. "I immediately thought better of it because they were unloading on me." Rounds were popping all around him, bouncing off the wall, ceiling, and floor. "I was very cognizant of the fact that I was standing at the end of someone else's firing range."

He shot off a few rounds into the room, but they were a feeble response to the barrage he had faced. He could not pinpoint where the shooters were, so he was just shooting aimlessly into the darkness. "It's a little hard to concentrate," Sanford said, "when there are two or three guys hosing you with AKs."

So Sanford scurried back down the hall and met up with the rest of the platoon waiting outside. They decided to throw a slew of grenades into the rooms hostile fire was coming from. But there was one problem: they had left the grenades back in the Strykers. They stood there, patting their pockets and searching for grenades, like suburbanites looking for car keys in the parking lot at the mall. "That felt really, really stupid," Sanford recalled. They eventually rounded up a few grenades, and one of the sergeants raced in the house to chuck the grenades at the enemy.

Sanford desperately wanted to see the grenades explode ("That's the fun part!"), so he peeked in the door and saw the sergeant throw them in the room at the end of the hall, sprint through the door past Sanford, and dive outside the house. Sanford turned his head back into the house to see the explosion. "Bad idea," he said. The blast from the grenades came back right at Sanford, with chunks of plaster and wood flying by his head. His face was peppered with dust and debris.

Right after the grenades, Sanford ran back into the house, with two of the sergeants following behind. They hadn't formulated any plans and were working off instinct. Sanford dashed down the hall to clear out the room with the two shooters. Unbeknownst to Sanford, the two sergeants had different plans—they went to the kitchen on the left to evacuate the wounded Americans.

Sanford proceeded to the end of the hallway and looked into the room on the right. That's when he appreciated the power of a grenade. He saw a man who had been ripped in half—his legs were strewn at an odd angle and his torso had been thrown to the side. He was just "unraveling intestines," Sanford recalled. Despite these mortal wounds, the man was dragging the upper half of his torso toward his AK-47, which lay a few feet away. As he saw him crawling to the weapon, Sanford shot him a few times. "He was going to die anyway and I was just being nice," Sanford explained. But then he quickly adds: "He still had about thirty seconds of life in him and he was going to use that to kill as many of us as possible."

Then he realized there was another guerrilla right next to him on his left. Sanford instantly started backpedaling around the corner out of the room and down the hall, trying to fire off a few rounds toward the insurgent. He had scurried about six feet down the hall when the insurgent pointed his AK-47 around the corner and unleashed a flurry of bullets at Sanford. "It was an ungodly amount of fire—probably an entire magazine of twenty to thirty rounds," Sanford remembered, shaking his head. "I felt little chunks of concrete popping off the hall all the way around me."

He backed up all the way to the entrance of the house. At that point, he decided he did not want to play nicely anymore. The shooting had largely tapered off, and he marched defiantly back toward the room. He stood in the hall and shot an entire magazine of thirty rounds into the wall on the other side of where the insurgent had been standing. The bullets eventually pierced through the wall, and then everything in the room became quiet.

Sanford then ran back outside and met up with the rest of the platoon. There, he saw the platoon leader, who been shot all over, including his shoulder and face. "He had goo running all over his face," Sanford recalled, recoiling at the image. The man could not speak, but was still leading the platoon and directing where to take casualties with an array of hand gestures and grunts. "That," Sanford said to himself, "is the bravest guy I have ever seen." The platoon leader would later receive a Silver Star for his actions that day.

Over the next few minutes, Sanford teamed up with two sergeants to evacuate the wounded Americans who remained trapped in the house. It was completely impromptu and they never planned a step, but everything just fell into place by instinct. Sanford entered the house first and provided cover as two of the sergeants darted in behind him to the kitchen to carry out their wounded comrades. "No one from our team," Sanford said with intense conviction, "was going to die in that house."

The three-man team went in and out of the house five or six times, with Sanford leading each time and providing suppressive fire as the sergeants carried guys out. By this point, Sanford said, he had switched into kill mode. "I can't tell you how many bullets I put down that hallway," he said, estimating that he unloaded hundreds of bullets in those trips. "I was shooting at everything hostile—if it wasn't American and it was in that house, I shot at it. If I had seen a sheep, I would have shot at it."

The kid from Michigan who played frog men and idolized warriors like Joe Beyrle was finally getting his chance at real action. "It was pretty exciting," he said, with boyish enthusiasm, "like the best Fourth of July show ever. Until you realize your buddies are getting killed and you get mad and you just want to kill everybody." Sanford insisted that he was totally in control of himself throughout the whole experience—he wasn't acting like a rabid animal with high-powered weaponry. To the contrary, he explained in a deliberative—albeit resigned—tone, "It was just 'I'm going to kill every single one of them.'"

Evacuating the wounded from inside the house proved tricky. Despite Sanford's voluminous covering fire, he received sporadic shooting from the insurgents. But more importantly, the conditions inside the house were awful. The combination of continual gunfire and explosions from grenades, mortars, and incendiary rounds—not to mention the resultant small fires dotted throughout the house—created a thick, heavy haze of smoke. Worse, the floor was drenched with the most blood Sanford had ever seen. "You couldn't walk because it was so slippery," Sanford recalled. "It was like if you poured motor oil all over the floor. So all of your weapons were bloody and hard to manipulate, you are losing your footing, and you're trying to pick [up] someone else who weighs more than you and they're wearing body armor and a boatload of ammo."

But the men persevered and safely evacuated all of the thirteen men who had been trapped in the house. Looking back on those moments, Sanford noted with evident pride that no Americans died in the house.

But, unfortunately, the insurgents were not done yet.

On one of the final trips, the two sergeants were pulling another sergeant out of the house. The man was in bad shape—he had grenade wounds to his head, along with multiple gunshot wounds. He was breathing, but he was unconscious. "He looked dead," Sanford remembered. One of the men who was under his command—Chris, the kid from Sanford's squad who had just gotten engaged—saw his team leader's condition and grew emotional, shouting incredulously that the man was dead. Sanford snapped at Chris, trying to get his friend to stop screaming. He was not actually angry with Chris, but the team leader was a popular guy and Sanford did not want the rest of the platoon to hear that he was dead because that would have destroyed everyone's morale. Also, Sanford liked the sergeant, and he just didn't want to hear that he was dead.

They were standing on the front step of the house, and Sanford urged Chris to go over to the Strykers sitting in the street by the remnants of the compound wall, which had been largely destroyed by this point. Sanford didn't really care where he went—he just wanted him to stop saying that the sergeant was dead.

Instead of going toward the right, in the direction that Sanford had motioned, Chris walked out in front of the house. He was completely exposed as he walked into the street. Then a shot rang out. Chris dropped instantly, shot in the neck.

Sanford was on the front step of the house, carrying one of the last injured soldiers out of the house, when he saw his buddy fall. Sanford dropped the guy that he was carrying ("We are still on speaking terms," Sanford insisted) and sprinted to help Chris, who was lying about forty feet away. As he reached his fallen friend, Sanford flung his rifle to his back like a rock star slinging a guitar out of the way. He dropped to the ground, with his knees straddling Chris's torso.

Sanford tried desperately to keep his friend alive. His EMT training kicked in as he threw a hand around Chris's neck to apply pressure to the wound and stanch the bleeding. He also started chest compressions with the other hand. The shooter was shooting at them, so Sanford was also trying to cover his friend with his own body as much as he could. "I was trying to do four or five things at once," Sanford said, with his voice quiet and choking up. "None of them were compatible." He was also screaming like a banshee for help, but virtually all of the platoon was occupied down the street with the dozen or so wounded men evacuated from the house.

Chris was lying in the street with the top of his head facing the house. Sanford, straddled on top of his friend's chest, was facing the house. Bullets pinged around them, but Sanford kept trying to save his buddy's life, pumping his chest with compressions and applying pressure to the wound. He saw bullets ricochet off of the street's pavement, with a few popping into his own vest. He knew bullets were hitting him, but "it was completely disregarded," Sanford recalled. He described his reaction as "Yep, I'm being shot," with a vocal inflection equivalent to a shoulder shrug. He was trying to save Chris's life, and everything else at that moment was secondary. "I've got better things to do than worry about pieces of metal sticking out of my vest."

So he continued giving his friend CPR for as long as he could. But then he felt an incredible impact on his leg. "It felt like I got hit in the groin with a baseball bat. And I don't mean like a T-ball bat—it was like Ken Griffey Jr. hitting you with a spiked club." He had gotten hit with a devastating shot in his upper thigh. He may have disregarded the other rounds that had hit him, but "I remember that one."

"That," Sanford said, "is when I started paying attention to the guy who was shooting at me." Sanford quickly realized that, if either he or Chris was going to survive, he had to kill the sniper. His leg hurt—badly—but he shifted his focus to killing the sniper. He described his thought process as "Ow, fuck! Now, kill him!" With that, Sanford said, his mind just switched off the pain.

He looked up to where the shots were coming from and saw the sniper in a window of the house about forty feet away. He was so close that Sanford could see the man's clothing and even his facial expressions. He was probably in his late twenties or early thirties, with short, dark hair. The man was clean-shaven and wore a green Adidas jumpsuit. And he was plugging away on his AK-47 right at Sanford.

Sanford reached his right hand around his back for his rifle and, in one fluid motion, flicked the safety button off and whipped the gun around. As he pulled the gun in front of him, he saw the red dot from his rifle's scope appearing right on the sniper's chest, shining brightly against the man's green sweatshirt. The muzzle flashes flared from the sniper's gun as he shot directly at Sanford. Sanford shot back, at first holding the gun with only one hand while the other applied pressure to his friend's neck. "I didn't want to let go," he said. The two men traded fire back and forth. "I'm shootin' him and I'm shootin' him and I'm shootin' him," Sanford recalled. "I shot him until I could not shoot him anymore." Sanford was sure that some of his shots were hitting the sniper, "but he had apparently not read the book that said that someone will stop shooting if you shoot them in the chest." Then—finally—the sniper stopped shooting. It was like a light switch had been turned off, and the man slumped over. Sanford would later learn that one of his shots had hit the shooter's upper spinal cord. "At that point, it was game over for him." The sniper was dead.

Sanford recalled shooting several shots before killing the man, and then everything blacked out. A number of his colleagues, though, told him later that he emptied a thirty-round magazine, loaded in a new magazine, and emptied the second before falling to the ground unconscious. He apparently kept firing—and even reloaded—after he blacked out.

Sanford recalled drifting in and out of consciousness as his platoon dragged him toward the Stryker to evacuate him, as well as the dozen or so other wounded men, to the hospital. Although his body was limp—he was bleeding profusely from the gunshot wound to his thigh—his mind was in an ethereal metastate, in which he was processing the whole situation and "triaging myself." Ever the EMT, Sanford went through the mental checklist of what he needed to do—treat his wound, apply pressure, monitor blood loss, and so on. Of course, he could do none of that, because he could barely move at all, but that was what was churning about in his mind. He recalled that the guys were dragging him backwards along the street, and the tip of the bullet lodged in his leg caught on the sidewalk. "Oh, that hurt," he said, contorting his face, reflecting the bitter memory. He unleashed a horrific scream as the bullet twisted around in his leg. "I didn't like that *at all.*" His comrades threw him in the Stryker and piled another wounded soldier on top of him. At some point, they thought Sanford was dead.

The Strykers formed a convoy and raced from the area shortly thereafter. They flew through the city, including running over parked cars, to get the wounded to the hospital as soon as possible. Sanford was drifting in and out of consciousness throughout the ride. He tried to keep his senses and actively keep himself alive, knowing about the extreme danger he faced if the bullet had severed his femoral artery. "Need pressure," his mind groaned plaintively, "need it now . . . femoral shot . . . going to bleed out."

This was the only time that Sanford felt in danger. "I was pretty sure I was going to die. It was game over for me." He wanted to say good-bye to the family. His leg ached badly, but he was in shock and started blocking it out, so he grew less aware of the pain. In his conscious moments, he was frustrated and mad at himself, with his inner voice muttering: "Damn it, why did you get shot, stupid?! Stupid, stupid, stupid." He was also worried about his friend Chris.

At one point during the ride, a massive twenty-five-pound machine gun, which was flopping around unsecured in the back of the Stryker, fell and landed with a thud on Sanford's chest. That woke him up. He looked up at the comrade who was in the air-guard position and said something like: "Pay attention—I won't make it. I enjoyed serving with you. Tell my wife I love her." According to Sanford, his friend used undiplomatic language to tell him to shut up. Then Sanford passed out again.

When the Stryker convoy arrived at hospital, the platoon started unloading the wounded guys. Sanford was toward the bottom of a large pile of wounded and bleeding infantrymen. By the time they got to Sanford, he heard one of the men say, "Shit—Sanford's dead." He was too weak to respond. The guy grabbed Sanford's vest and started dragging him out to get to the survivors below. As he pulled Sanford, "that damn bullet got caught again," and Sanford let out another primal scream of pain. "Oh, shit—Sanford's alive!"

He was rushed into the emergency room. He knew they would intubate him and, for some reason, he did not want to be intubated. He recalled yelling at the doctors: "Don't intubate me!" The last thing he remembered as he passed out, however, was the staff intubating him. "The bastards did it anyway," he said.

Sanford woke up at some point the next day. He learned later that he had multiple cardiac arrests during surgery and the defibrillators brought him back each time.

His sergeant came to visit him that day. Sanford said that his first thought was that the sergeant was going to yell at him because he left a few magazines at the battle scene, which they are instructed not to do. As he walked in the room, the sergeant said: "All right, Sanford, it's time to go back to work." Sanford responded with an earnest: "Yes, First Sergeant!" He started getting up out of the bed, ready to go. The self-proclaimed worst soldier in the history of the US Army, who couldn't care less about Army rules, all of a sudden wanted to pop up for a proper military greeting. "I'm sorry, First Sergeant!" he said as he struggled to stand up. But his leg gave out, and he fell flat on his face.

Apparently, Sanford still could not quite get the Army Way. But this time, he at least had a good excuse.

Sanford later learned that the firefight on that day would continue for another twelve hours. News accounts of the firefight reported that US and Iraqi officials said coalition forces had received a tip that al-Qaeda leader Abu Musab al-Zarqawi was meeting with senior deputies at the house and that the fierce resistance by fighters heightened suspicions that Zarqawi might have been inside.

Sanford believed that he killed two to four insurgents during the firefight. He was proud of the fact that the Army confirmed at least one of them, a rare feat for a private. In fact, he became the first private in his brigade to earn a confirmed kill.

Two American soldiers were killed during the firefight—Sanford's buddy Chris and a Special Forces soldier who became involved after Sanford had been evacuated. Sanford felt guilty about what happened with his friend. Years later, Sanford would get choked up thinking about it for just a fleeting moment. "Obviously I did something wrong." On some level, he recognized that no one knew a sniper was lurking in the house and "lining up that one-in-a-million, golden shot." It was a perfect angle, Sanford recalled—no trees, no obstructive rubble. "Chris just happened to walk across the sight line. And the shot to the neck, rather than his vest or his helmet? That's one in a million." Still, Sanford said, guilt still ate away at him.

Chris's death devastated the Alcozer family, said his half brother Jesse. Worse, it was part of a series of events so tragic that it garnered national attention. The month before Chris's death, his father—a former Marine who had been wounded seven times in Vietnam—saw his veteran's benefits cut by 20 percent, leaving the family in a precarious financial condition. The Department of Veterans Affairs threatened to further reduce his benefits by 80 percent. "My father had shrapnel all over him—and bullet wounds too," Jesse said, "and they were taking away his benefits."

The firefight in Mosul occurred just a few weeks later. During Chris's funeral, half a dozen protesters staged a demonstration against the war. As family and friends mourned inside the church, the demonstrators stood across the street carrying signs that read "Thank God for Dead Soldiers." Their presence infuriated Chris's family. "They had no right to be there," Jesse said. "I don't care what you're protesting. To show up at a funeral carrying your signs, it was wrong. 'How *dare* you?!'" he asked rhetorically. "I was carrying the casket—if I wasn't a pallbearer, I would've gone over there and shared a piece of my mind." At the same time, Jesse felt sorry for them. "I don't understand their mentality, so you have to pity them."

And, Jesse said, his brother would have taken the high road. "Chris had such a good heart, he would've just laughed at them. He had so much positive energy in him. He would have laughed and asked, 'You have nothing better to do?'" Jesse said, brightening at the thought of Chris's hypothetical reaction. "He was so *good*."

Enduring "hateful" and "hurtful" jeers from protesters during a relative's funeral would be a low point for anyone, but the Shakespearean tragedy would get worse for the Alcozer family. They had set up a shrine in his father's house to honor Chris's memory, featuring the flag that had been draped over his coffin, pictures from his life, and several memorial candles. On December 27, 2005, just two days after Christmas and only five weeks after Chris's funeral, one of the candles started a fire. Although the family, who had been watching a movie upstairs, escaped unharmed, the blaze destroyed the house.

But all was not lost. The fire somehow circled around the shrine, Jesse said, leaving the flag and Chris's medals intact. A firefighter ran through the fire to grab them and return them to the family. "In light of all the damage and heartache," Jesse recalled, "the fact that the physical memorials of Chris were safe was amazing." He took that, and the fact that no one was injured, as a message from God. "It was a blessing that every-one was safe. It was God's way of saying, 'Despite the tragedy, everyone is safe.' No matter what your faith, God does things for a reason. He takes his angels. To have the shrine untouched, amidst a fire, that was awesome. You just have to smile. Every-thing else can be replaced."

News of the Alcozers' dire situation spread quickly, and the community came together to help the family. The lieutenant governor of the state, who had spoken at Chris's funeral and was outraged at the protesters' antics, established a fund to help the family, and donations poured in from citizens around the country. "We received hundreds and hundreds and hundreds of letters," Jesse recalled, struggling to convey the enormity of the response. "I mean *hundreds* of letters. People sent donations large and small." Local companies donated a house, furniture, and moving services to help the family. In March 2006, only a few months after the fire, the Alcozers moved into their new house, located less than a mile from their old home.

"It was so surreal," Jesse said of the community's response to their calamities. "It was beautiful." This was a silver lining to the terrible dark cloud over their family, Jesse said. He also finds comfort in Chris's memory. "He died a hero. He was—and al-ways will be—my angel," Jesse said. "I know he's gone upstairs. I know he's with our other family and he's waiting for us."

Sanford spent months recovering from his wounds and had to learn how to walk again. He spent time at Walter Reed Army

Medical Center, which provided "phenomenal" care. He also marveled at the effort from personnel in the combat hospital in Iraq—the "bastards" that had intubated him over his vehement objections. "I really should thank them for the eighteen hours of work they put into what everyone knew was a lost cause. There is no medical reason that I can think of that I should have lived."

He was medically discharged from the Army after his recovery, but he wanted to return to Iraq to finish the job. "I will go back if they ask me," he said months before US troops pulled out of the country. And then he added with a deadpan: "They won't ask." But if they did, Sanford described his response: "'Woo-hoo!' I'd be on the first plane outta here." His wife shook her head as he said that, and he added: "She knows there is nothing she can do to stop me. The job is not done. Al-Qaeda is still out there."

The platoon received a truckload of medals and commendations for its actions during the firefight. The 172nd Stryker Brigade Combat Team was awarded the Valorous Unit citation, and numerous soldiers received Silver Stars, Purple Hearts, Bronze Star Medals, and Army Commendation Medals.

Sanford received the highest medal in the platoon, a Distinguished Service Cross, which is second only to the Medal of Honor. General Peter Pace, then chairman of the Joint Chiefs of Staff, the highest-ranking military officer in the United States, traveled to Alaska so that he could personally pin the medal on Sanford's chest. During the ceremony, General Pace told the audience that, while he had participated in many award ceremonies, "this is the first time I have ever had the honor of awarding a Distinguished Service Cross." Sanford recalled that the general's hands shook slightly as he pinned the medal on his chest. Pace apologized to him, saying: "Sorry, this is the first time I've given one of these out." Sanford, ever the jokester, responded: "Don't worry, General, it's my first one too."

Sanford said that he cannot be objective about whether his actions were heroic. When he thinks of heroism, he imagines someone doing something extraordinarily difficult and putting a great burden on himself. "For me to say that it was difficult and I knowingly endangered my life, it's nonsense because I didn't knowingly put my life in danger. I knew I was in danger, but I didn't care. I've always been a push-it-to-the-limit kind of guy. It's the Warrior Ethos: 'I will always put the mission first; I will never accept defeat; and I will never leave a fallen comrade behind.' That's it, right there. We did not. We did not accept defeat, and we did not leave behind fallen comrades."

Sanford bristled when real heroes demur and say they were just doing their jobs. He mentioned World War II medics who scaled cliffs forty to fifty times to pull down injured comrades. "That wasn't your job!" Sanford said incredulously. "You scaled a cliff *with a body!*" Those were real heroes—guys who did much more than what their jobs required—guys like Joe Beyrle and Chuck Yeager. In contrast, he viewed the moments of his firefight as very different—he believed he was just doing his job. "That's what I was paid to do. Now," he added with his mischievous smirk, "you can argue about the equity of my pay for that task."

Perhaps Sanford will call his union representative to file a grievance.

Larry "Buck" Doyle flying in a UH-60 Black Hawk helicopter over Kunar province, Afghanistan, as a civilian consultant after his retirement from the US Marine Corps. Courtesy of Buck Doyle.

Buck Doyle
Eternal Love of the Brotherhood

The video starts with a black page filled with Arabic writing. The letters are blood red, contrasting sharply against the dark, ominous background. Arabic music, upbeat and seemingly celebratory, blares in the background. A computerized black flag adorned with Arabic writing—a symbol associated with fundamentalist terrorist groups—waves at the top of the screen. Below the flag sits a large insignia with crossed crescents, a spear, and an open book.

After a few seconds, the graphics dissolve, and the video jumps to a shaky recording from a handheld camera. The screen shows two busy highways baking under the bright Middle Eastern sun, one in the immediate foreground and the other, one hundred meters back. As traffic crosses the screen close by, the camera focuses on a group of American Marines located on the far highway. There are nine or ten men, all wearing full combat gear and standing between several military Humvees and a tow truck. They are milling around, talking with each other casually in small clumps of two or three. They seem unaware that they are being watched.

The video stays focused on the Marines for a few seconds. Then the image shakes dramatically, jerking up and then slamming down. As it stabilizes, the video shows one of the Americans crumpling lifelessly to the ground. The others scatter instantly—all but one of them. He stays in place and reaches down to the fallen man, while the others dart away, scurrying for cover behind the trucks nearby. Standing exposed on the highway—where his colleague was just shot—he works hurriedly to get a grip on the man's camouflage gear and help him.

As he stands above the fallen soldier, the image flickers up and down again. The standing Marine whirls around and falls in a heap by his injured colleague. A third American, who had come over to help, darts for cover behind a nearby Humvee.

After a brief pause, the third man comes out from behind the truck, going back into the line of fire. He extends his arms and grabs one of the fallen men, tugging and pulling the man backward behind the Humvee. The camera shakes violently again, and the video ends.

Arabic words scrolling on the bottom of the screen offer praise to Allah and celebrate the killing of three Americans.

Buck Doyle is the quintessential "gunny," the respect-laden term given to gunnery sergeants in the US Marine Corps. Gunnies are the Marines' grizzled veterans, the senior noncommissioned officers who have seen and done everything, and Doyle is straight out of central casting. He had deployed overseas numerous times, served in the USMC's elite Force Reconnaissance unit, was a Marine Corps scout sniper, was part of the prewar operation that paved the way for the first wave of Marines in the 2003 invasion of Iraq, and spent time serving as a drill instructor, platoon sergeant, and lead instructor at the First Special Operations Training Group. "There isn't a situation I haven't been in, in a combat environment," he said. "Starving on a battlefield, getting shot, getting blown up, helicopters crashing—I've been there, done that."

At an early age, Doyle knew he would join the military. The first Rambo movie, he said, captivated him. "*First Blood* really got my interest going in Special Forces and stuff like that," he said. "It's when I was ten years old. From that day, my interest was sparked to be a Rambo guy." But his attraction to the military was founded on more than just a single movie. He grew up a "military brat" whose father spent his entire career in the Army. He felt comfortable in the military environment. "It's what I knew," he said. "Growing up, my father got up, put his fatigues on, and went to work. He came home sweating. I saw him in formation. So I was familiar with that whole environment, that whole lifestyle. If you were to say, 'Be a businessman or a carpenter,' that was all foreign."

After graduating from high school, Doyle enlisted in the military. Although his father was a career Army man, Doyle opted for the Marines. He wanted to conduct reconnaissance missions, going behind enemy lines like Rambo, and he believed the Marines would best develop the special recon skill set. He began his service in the infantry, biding his time until he could join one of the elite reconnaissance units.

His quest to become a recon Marine received a huge boost during a deployment in the first war with Iraq. He was part of a standby force that was stationed on a ship in the Persian Gulf and, although he saw no combat, he met three Marines who would change his life. The men were part of the select Force Reconnaissance unit, commonly called Force Recon. One of the Marines' Special Forces groups, Force Recon is analogous to the Navy SEALs or the military's other special operations teams. The three Force Recon Marines—who went by the call signs Frog, Ripper, and Hermy—mentored the young lance corporal in the art of Marine reconnaissance. "They broke down every intricacy of navigation, marksmanship, fieldcraft, *everything*," he recalled. "They broke it down into so much detail that it opened my eyes." He pointed to their guidance on navigation as an example. "Navigation was more than having a compass, but how to read the degrees, how to do the computations of where you're at, reading stars." Their teaching went far beyond technical skills. "They worked out with me, and they pushed me. These guys were phenomenal, like professional athletes. They wore me out.

I understood what it means to feel pain and the dedication that it takes to get in shape."

Besides the incredible training with Frog, Ripper, and Hermy, Doyle watched the Force Recon unit conduct two missions, including boarding and seizing a supertanker illegally entering the Persian Gulf waters. He witnessed them planning and preparing for the operations, and then watched through binoculars from the bow of his ship as they executed them. He saw Force Recon Marines board the ship from the bow while others slid down ropes from helicopters to the ship's deck, all while Iraqis on the tanker shot water cannons at them.

Watching the Force Recon unit conduct missions, Doyle said, "strengthened my testimony that what I was shooting for is attainable. I was actually able to witness people I know execute the dream I wanted to fulfill. It's like anything else—if you have a goal to go to school and get that degree, and you go to graduation your freshman year and watch people walk across the stage—it means 'Man, I can do that.' In my line of work, to see someone do a mission, it is probably never going to happen until you do it, so you're always going to be wondering. I no longer had to wonder—I had seen it from A to Z."

Doyle's experience with the Force Recon guys was a huge turning point in his career and a real dream come true. "It was priceless to be able to sit there and engage with those guys on a daily basis." Through all of their mentoring and watching their missions, Doyle realized that becoming a recon Marine "was not going to be an overnight thing," he said. "It's going to take lots of dedication, lots of time to become an adequate reconnaissance Marine. It takes about three minutes to look like a recon Marine, but it takes about ten years to become one."

Doyle was ready to start that process. Before the end of that deployment, he had scheduled a date to take the Force Recon indoctrination test.

The Force Recon indoctrination program, Doyle recalled, was "six and a half weeks of hell." They woke up every day at 4:30 in the morning for about two hours of physical fitness, like calisthenics and hiking. They trained extensively on every aspect of reconnaissance work—concealment, navigation, communications, and swimming and amphibious work in both pools and open water. Instructors constantly monitored their progress and tested them repeatedly. He recalled tedious navigation tests, in which they had to use grid coordinates and a compass to locate a three-foot stake buried in the middle of some bush miles away.

The arduous training instilled a powerful bond among the trainees, which was different from the bond Doyle had developed over his four years in the infantry. "When you're sitting on a beach freezing—and I mean literally *freezing*—and all you have is three other guys, you guys all have to come together and spoon to stay warm—you're going to become close real quick." But the bond was deeper than mere survival; these men were so committed that they would do anything for each other. "In those situations, you give up *everything*—you have to, or you will die. They have to know your fears, your deepest fears, your deepest concerns. In forty-five days, you talk about them probably more than if you were married for ten to twenty years, with a guy you just met a month ago."

The experience had a profound impact on Doyle. Although he had enlisted to be "a Rambo guy," Doyle's interests matured with the Force Recon indoctrination. "Every day, you put your head down and ask yourself, 'Why am I doing this?!' You're asking yourself that because you're tired, you have blisters on your feet, you have a rash that you got somewhere in a forest with poison oak, and it won't go away, and you're irritating it. You may have hit your face on the zodiac boat. You're worried about failing. There are a lot of things going on physically and mentally," he recalled. "And you look up in your hooch, and you have six to nine guys thinking the same thing you are. At the end of the day, you are doing it because of the *camaraderie*," he said with growing passion. "You know that, if you individually excel and are successful on your own, you will be able to contribute to a four- to six-man team and be *unstoppable*. And that's when I knew it wasn't me becoming Rambo to do everything by *myself*. It was me becoming Rambo to make a *team*."

The bond, Doyle said, is unbreakable and as addictive as a narcotic. "The effort and the dedication that each individual puts out every day just to make sure your buddy is going to be okay or your buddy is going to succeed is *brotherly love*. It's hard to define it, it's hard to explain to someone what it feels like, but it's *phenomenal*," he said. "It's a high like no other. I tell my wife all the time, 'If there wasn't a certain need from a woman, I would probably just stay in the Marine Corps with a bunch of guys,'" he said with a hearty laugh.

That bond—Doyle's willingness to do anything for his fellow Marines—would be tested on a busy Iraqi highway on May 26, 2007.

Before sunrise that morning, Doyle was preparing for yet another mission near Fallujah, Iraq. Since his indoctrination into Force Recon in 1991, Doyle had risen nicely through the enlisted ranks, eventually being promoted to gunnery sergeant. In 2005, Doyle became the senior noncommissioned officer in a platoon of twenty-four reconnaissance Marines. It was a dream job for the gunny, as it was the most senior enlisted position that still operated out in the field. Anything more senior, he said, and he would be relegated to an office somewhere. At that point, he said, "your time of being in the bush and gettin' after it are over."

As the platoon sergeant, Doyle's role transformed. At thirty-five years old, Doyle was the old man of the platoon. He became a father figure to the men in his platoon, most of whom were novice Marines at least a decade younger than him. As a young Marine, he said, "I was riding a high just on my physical attributes—my ability to suck it up when it really sucked and still execute, my ability to shoot, my ability to send Morse code when I can't feel my fingers, my ability to brief a two-star general when you're twenty-two years old. It's a high. As you get older, you are given more responsibility—you're in charge of more of your brothers and you're older than them. And you realize: 'I've got to take care of *everyone*.'"

Doyle relished the role and developed special relationships with his men. The bond grew tight as the platoon deployed to Iraq in August 2005 through February 2006. They conducted numerous patrols and engaged with the enemy in a handful of firefights. His men had performed well, and he was proud of them. Most importantly, he said, "everyone came home without a scratch. It was a very good deployment."

The platoon returned to Iraq for its second deployment in February 2007, as part of the American surge. They were stationed at Camp Fallujah, a midsize American base outside the city of the same name. The first four months of the deployment were more active—"a lot more kinetic," Doyle said—than the first tour in Iraq. While they were ostensibly housed at Camp Fallujah, Doyle spent far more time out in the field than at the base. The longest stretch he stayed at the base was three days. Out in the field with his men, the gunny was a happy man.

In the predawn hours of May 26, 2007, however, Doyle was a little on edge. Their mission that day was to scout an area for a countersniper operation. An insurgent marksman had recently targeted a nearby outpost and hit one or two Marines. Doyle's platoon was responsible for finding and eliminating the sniper. His first step was to survey the area and see what they could do to support the outpost. Normally, they would conduct such a scouting mission, especially when a sniper is lurking, under the cover of night. This was an urgent problem, however, and they were directed to leave that morning.

So Doyle assembled a small group, including his three team leaders and the platoon's snipers, to search the area. They left the base before dawn in a four-Humvee caravan, proceeding out of the main entrance to the base and onto one of the main highways leading east toward Fallujah. Doyle's right-hand man, a sergeant named Nick Walsh, was in the lead Humvee. Doyle rode in the last vehicle, about five hundred meters behind. The highway was completely flat, with large swaths of barren desert straddling the road. Traffic was light in those early morning hours, and they encountered only a smattering of cars and trucks on the road.

Roughly fifteen minutes into their trip, however, Doyle received a distressing call on the radio. The lead Humvee—Sergeant Walsh's vehicle—had been in an accident. An Iraqi car had collided with the Humvee, wrecking the vehicle's front differential and rendering it inoperable.

This was exactly what Doyle was afraid of in conducting a daytime mission. It was much worse than simply repairing a broken part. Protocol required that they could not continue the mission—they had to remain with the broken-down vehicle and wait for a tow-truck crew to haul it back to the base. That, Doyle knew, could take hours. In the meantime, Doyle and his mates would be stuck—exposed like sitting ducks—in the middle of the day with few options for cover.

Wary of a sniper or a vehicle-borne IED, Doyle directed the team to take preventative measures. First, he told everyone to stay in their vehicles. He also instructed them to extend their perimeter. "We were all jammed up together," he recalled, "so we pushed out and widened our space." He sent one of the Humvees three hundred meters ahead of the broken-down vehicle (toward the east) and directed another to secure the perimeter about three hundred meters back (to the west). This, he said, created "a large bubble to have vantage points" of the surrounding area and mitigated the threat of a vehicle bomb. Doyle rode in the remaining operable Humvee, driving up and down the scene to make sure everything and everyone was okay. The men stayed in their vehicles and scanned the area through binoculars for threats. Each Humvee also had a man in the gun turret, manning the massive fifty-caliber Barrett rifles and surveying the area for suspicious activity.

As they waited for the tow-truck personnel, called a wrecker crew, the morning ripened around them: the sun started to blaze in the clear sky, and the highway began coming to life. Despite the increasing activity around them, Doyle and his men had no choice but to wait. The delay was excruciating. Hours passed as they remained stalled on the highway. Doyle feared that local insurgents must have learned of the broken-down American caravan and were hurriedly maneuvering to take advantage of the situation.

Finally, around noon—hours after the accident—a wrecker crew finally arrived at the scene. Rather than being blessed salvation, the new arrivals irritated the gunny. There was a miscommunication between Doyle's team and the wrecker crew. Doyle had expected them to call before they approached the scene, so they could prepare strategically. The wrecker crew comprised four Humvees and a civilian flatbed tow truck, and the gunny wanted to string the Humvees from his unit and the wrecker crew on both sides of the road, creating a massive screen so that the tow truck could load the broken Humvee without fear of a sniper attack.

But the wrecker crew didn't telegraph their approach, and their arrival created tactical problems in Doyle's eyes. The vehicles were "all jammed up," Doyle said colorfully, "all belly button–to–butt." The Humvees were packed together around the broken-down truck, forming a big target and minimizing their individual flexibility. Worse, he saw the Marines from the wrecker crew get out of their vehicles and congregate around the busted Humvee.

Doyle directed the driver in his Humvee to head toward the wrecker—the former drill instructor wanted to give them a piece of his mind. "My plan," he said, "was to drive up and get everyone back in the trucks and reorganize, recock, and start all over again." As his Humvee flew back toward the bunched-up wrecker vehicles, Doyle saw the tow-truck operators, two civilians with potbellies and extraordinarily long beards, sauntering around the wrecked Humvee "like they're back home in Texas." The sight of the two ZZ Top look-alikes cracked him up, despite his irritation. "I was laughing and pissed at the same time," he conceded with a hint of a smile.

But the situation was serious, and Doyle grew increasingly annoyed as his Humvee drove westward toward the wreck. It was, he feared, a perfect scenario for an insurgent strike.

Upon arriving at the crowd of wrecker-crew Marines, Doyle hopped out of his vehicle. Then he "commenced chewing butt," telling the new arrivals to get back in their trucks. As Doyle tried to corral the Marines, Nick Walsh, his right-hand man who had been waiting in the broken-down Humvee, jumped down to the street to help his gunny.

This was typical of Walsh, Doyle said. "He was really my go-to guy. If a crappy situation came up, he would say, 'I'll do it, gunny. Don't worry about it.'" The two men had developed a strong relationship ever since the gunny had become platoon sergeant three years earlier. "You can fall in love with Nick real quick," Doyle said. "Everyone loved him." He was the platoon jokester, always with a great story at the ready.

Beyond his social graces, though, Walsh was a gifted leader and a valuable resource for the gunny. "I was not touchy in dealing with the guys," Doyle said. Walsh was, and he helped Doyle communicate with the men effectively. "He would convey [my] command in a way that everyone else could understand. That was a gift that Nick had."

Doyle also respected Walsh as a reconnaissance Marine. He came from a long pedigree of distinguished military service, which Doyle said made him who he was—beneath his affable personality was a kid who was raised by patriots, believed in what he was doing, and was willing to die for his country. The two men had fought in numerous combat engagements during their deployments in both 2005 and 2007. "He was a very good teammate," Doyle said. "He did it all, and we did it all together. I probably did more missions with him than I've done collectively with a lot of the Marines I know." Under fire, Doyle said, "Nick was a smooth operator." He recalled Walsh's performance during one particularly fierce ambush in the 2005 deployment. "Our whole firebase [was] getting ambushed. I was giving him commands, and he was fighting back, driving, and getting hit with IEDs," Doyle said. "He was a cool, calm operator." Walsh was more than Doyle's right-hand man—he was essentially a brother.

So it didn't surprise Doyle that Walsh would help him corral the men from the wrecker crew. "By the time I got out and started yelling, Nick—*naturally*—got out because he saw his gunny out there, chewin' ass, so he wanted to get out there and help out."

As Doyle and Walsh worked to organize the other Marines, a couple of other officers gathered near Walsh's broken-down vehicle. The men exchanged pleasantries for the briefest of moments.

And then a shot rang out.

Doyle heard the shot. It sounded like a crack from the practice range. It impacted something nearby. Walsh yelled out, "I'm hit!" as his legs gave out, and he slumped to the ground. Everyone scattered, darting for cover by the nearby vehicles.

Everyone, that is, except for the gunny.

Standing an arm's length from where Walsh was shot, Doyle stayed put. His right-hand man—his *brother*—was hurt, and Doyle wasn't going to leave him alone. He understood that he was standing squarely in the sniper's range, but he was determined to help Walsh and pull him out of the sniper's fire. Doyle's truck was only a few feet behind them, and he thought it would provide them cover.

He bent down, his left hand outstretched. Another round cracked through the air. This time, the crack of the round seemed right in front of him, almost feeling like a puff of wind brushing against his face.

His gloved hand struggled momentarily to get a grip on Walsh's uniform. As Doyle worked feverishly, Walsh was lying on his back looking up and trying to talk. He seemed to be pointing out where the shooter was. "He said a few other things, but it was hard to make out," Doyle said.

Doyle heard the sniper's rifle pop for a third time. He felt a thud—he knew the round had hit him, but he didn't know where. He was focused on pulling Walsh out of the sniper fire, and the injury wasn't stopping him, so he just kept pulling.

As Doyle got a grip on the left shoulder strap on the front of Walsh's vest, one of the officers scampered toward the gunny and grabbed Walsh by the other shoulder. As the men started to yank backwards, Doyle noticed that Walsh's movements had slowed down. Then he went quiet.

By then, the sniper was zeroing in on them. A few seconds later, the rifle spat out a fourth shot.

The bullet struck Doyle just above his left elbow. "It felt like a thud," Doyle recalled, "like someone taking a rubber mallet and hitting you in the arm." The force spun him around clockwise and threw him to the ground. He was dizzy and disoriented, like someone had punched him in the nose. "I had that out-of-body experience when you just got your bell rung," he said. "In my head, I was trying to say, 'Let's go, let's go, let's go!' but I couldn't."

He looked down at his arm and couldn't believe what he saw. The bullet had entered about two inches above his elbow and had come out the other side, taking out about one-third of his left bicep. His arm below the wound was flopping around uncontrollably. "It was like a nunchuck, like a Muppet, just going wherever," he recalled. "Imagine your [shirt] being twisted like there's nothing in it, like someone was wringing your [sleeve] out. So I was trying to figure out which way to turn my arm without screwing it up more. I was trying to figure out this Rubik's Cube: 'Do I turn it left? Do I turn it right?'" Twisting his arm didn't hurt, the gunny said, "but it wasn't pleasant either— you could feel your bones crushing and grinding."

As Doyle lay on the ground trying to fix his arm, the officer picked him up from behind and dove backwards into the closest Humvee. They landed in a heap in the backseat of the vehicle, with the gunny situated on his right side on top of the officer. Space was tight, and neither man could move. "Two guys in the back of a Humvee," Doyle said, "would have been hard on a normal day."

As the officer worked to strap a tourniquet around the gunny's injured arm, Doyle became alarmed as he realized that they were in the Walsh's broken-down truck. "We gotta get out of here," he thought to himself. "This is *wrong*—we can't be in this vehicle." Not only did they have to get out of that particular Humvee, he said, they had to get out of the kill zone. "We were still in the impact area, and I knew I needed to get out of there. That's when the training starts to kick in," he said, adding as if reading out of a military instruction manual: "*Get out of the impact area.*"

As Doyle tried to clear his head, another Humvee raced over to evacuate him. It screeched to a stop next to the Humvee's open door, facing west and screening off the kill zone from the shooter, who was likely perched to the north. The Marines in the other vehicle had popped smoke grenades, which billowed a thick purple smoke to cloud the enemy's view and give the men some space to evacuate the gunny. A couple of Marines hopped out and started pulling Doyle into an evacuation vehicle, while the platoon medic and another Marine loaded Walsh into a different Humvee.

Once the gunny was inside the new Humvee, it raced off, heading west toward Camp Fallujah. "We were NASCAR-ing it," Doyle recalled. "We were hauling butt."

As the Humvee took off toward Camp Fallujah, Doyle sat in the backseat, on the passenger side. His head was still cloudy. "I was trying to get my bearings—I just got my bell rung." But, as he struggled to break through the cobwebs, he understood the impact his injury could have on his men and knew that it was imperative that he remain in control. "I'm the gunny—there's probably a ten- to fifteen-year difference in age. I was thirty-seven and the oldest guy in there was probably twenty-six or twenty-seven," he explained. "When I got into the new vehicle, I had four or five Marines looking at me asking what do we do. But they're also seeing their gunny shot." So Doyle barked out commands to his men, making sure the situation did not degenerate on the ride to the base triage center. "To this day, I still don't remember everything I said or did during that time," he said.

"A lot of things were happening that training can't fully prepare you for mentally or physically," he said. "It was just a lot of unknowns. I was asking myself questions inside, [and] at the same time, trying to figure out what was going on. 'Where's Nick? Was Nick dead?' I think at that time I knew Nick had passed, but I didn't want to believe it yet."

He could see through the windshield another Humvee in front of them racing toward the base. Walsh was lying in the open-air payload of that truck, with the platoon medic treating him. "My questions were answered when I looked in front of me and saw that vehicle and was told Doc was in there working on Nick." Doyle could hear over the vehicle's radio that Walsh was being treated and was headed for the emergency room. But, he said, "I think I knew internally—I knew where he got hit. I just knew from experience about guys getting shot and not making it. I knew it wasn't good."

His head also swirled about his own injury. "The whole time I didn't know whether I was dying," he said. "We had always talked about death and those scenarios, but no one ever said: 'This is what you'll feel like when you're dying,' or 'When you've lost too much blood, you're getting ready to die,' or 'This is what your heart feels like when you're getting ready to pass away.' So I was sitting there, I got shot and I had all this blood on me, and I was going through a mental check on all my vitals, like 'Okay, I'm breathing normally.' I was trying to figure out what state I was in. I was still barking out commands, but at that point reality kicked in, and it was like 'You've just been *shot*, dummy.' Up to this point, I thought I was Superman, but I just got introduced to Kryptonite."

He was not concerned with physical pain—or even death itself—but rather with the uncertainty of the situation. "I just got shot, I had a tourniquet on me, I lost blood, I had all these chemicals going through my body—I was going through it for the first time and it's for real—there is no practice. That's the fear of *not knowing*," he said. "Because you can't train for that. You can train to a degree, but when you get there, you gotta hope everything else about you—your *character*—will be what you *hope* it is."

Next to Doyle in the backseat sat one of his team leaders, who was cranking the tourniquet on Doyle's arm to stem the bleeding. "This guy was probably six foot two, 220 pounds," Doyle recalled. "He *crushed* my arm. That's what brought me back to reality, because the pain kicked in real quick. He's a strong kid, and he was cranking down on that thing, twisting with all that leverage. And it hurt like hell."

The Humvees arrived back at the camp within about ten to fifteen minutes and took Doyle and Walsh directly to the hospital. Over the ensuing weeks, Doyle endured multiple surgeries at hospitals around the world. The operations addressed wounds from the shot to the arm, but also one in the leg. "I didn't know," Doyle said, of the shot to his leg. He found out later that one of the sniper's shots had hit the side plate of his body armor, ricocheted down his armor to his groin plate, and went into his leg. The surgeries and the recovery process were not pleasant. "It was horrible," he said. "It sucked." But he learned to appreciate the value of the pain medication. "I was high as a kite for about six days."

Roughly two days after the shooting, insurgents posted a video of the event on the Internet, incorrectly boasting that three Americans had been killed in the attack. It was a short propaganda film, with shaky camerawork and unsophisticated graphics. But putting out the video might have been the insurgents' biggest mistake—it put a huge target on their backs, and the recon Marines wanted revenge. "Our two platoons did a *hunt* for these guys," Doyle said. He had been in and out of surgery and shuttled to hospitals around the world, but Doyle heard about his company's efforts to track the sniper. The video helped out a lot, he said. Eight days after the shooting, the Marines got their man. "It was very ironic for them because it was a sniper mission back on them. One of our recon teams got him on a bad day."

Doyle understood the value in killing the sniper featured in a propaganda video. "It was good from a tactical perspective because the guy was bragging about this. And we were able to use information operations to say: 'Hey, your guy went out and did this to our guy—look where he is now.' From a strategic piece, from an operational piece, it was good," he said. He quickly added, "But it was also satisfying to know that that guy is gone. There was satisfaction across the board. I was happy as hell."

Buck Doyle received a Bronze Star Medal with Combat Distinguishing Device for attempting to save Sergeant Walsh's life. The commendation, however, baffles him. "What happened that day with Nick, at the end of the day, I failed as a leader. I came back minus one of my guys—I'm in charge, I failed," he said. "The way I think, for someone to grant me an award for that makes no damn sense. That award is for Nick. It's not even an appropriate award. The fact that I failed and Nick is gone—I don't understand how you associate any kind of award for that."

Doyle bristled at the idea of honors and commendations in general, saying that his fulfillment comes not from ribbons or medals. "I don't really think about awards *at all*. You do your job, and if you have the opportunity to go above and beyond your duties, then that's the reward in itself," he said. "The award for me is the *brotherhood*. If you are accepted in that brotherhood, that's the greatest award you can receive. For me, my award is having Nick's parents regard me as part of their family—that's a *huge* award. Hearing the story that Nick spoke of me the whole time to his parents, that he regarded me as a brother. That is the eternal reward that no colonel can think about giving me, so I regard that responsibility and honor of serving with those guys as the award."

Looking back on the incident, Doyle believes it was that brotherly love that motivated him to risk his life to try to save Walsh's. Although Marines are trained to address a threat first and then take care of casualties, "subconsciously, I always knew I would never do that. I always knew I would go out there and grab a brother. Because the last thing I would ever want was to have someone die alone," he said, his voice trembling and barely audible over his tears. "I've always practiced and trained the guys to finish the fight and take care of the threat, and then you take care of the casualty, but you're just not going to do that in real life with someone you love—it's easy to say and do that in training, but when it's a brother, you are going to act off of love. And that's what happened."

That love compelled Doyle to recover from his injuries—and return to the battlefield. "I told the doctor: 'Doc, I need you to fix my arm so I can go back out there.'" He endured multiple surgeries and extensive rehabilitation, but stayed focused on the goal of returning to combat yet again. In August 2009, roughly two years after the shooting that nearly killed him, Doyle deployed to Afghanistan for another combat tour. He served for another three and a half years in the Marines after the May 2007 incident, and was promoted to master sergeant.

"People ask, 'Why do you do it?'" he said. "At the end of the day, it's for your brother. You're not going to let him go out there in harm's way by himself—you're *going*. There's no question. As long as there's a war, somehow, someway, I'm going to be out there." He emphasized that he is not a crazed warmonger. "No, I just fell in love with the brotherhood, and it's not going away. It's eternal."

Chris Kyle receiving the Grateful Nation Award from the Jewish Institute for National Security Affairs (JINSA) on December 12, 2005. Courtesy of JINSA.

Chris Kyle
The Overworked Guardian Angel

As he ran up the dusty alley in a godforsaken corner of Fallujah, Chris Kyle believed he was about to die. The Navy SEAL sniper was dragging an injured Marine toward a safe house fifty yards away. But a handful of insurgents had other plans—plans that didn't include Kyle and his charge reaching the house alive. The guerrillas were chasing him up the alley, shooting at him from less than thirty yards away. It was essentially point-blank. Kyle thought he had no chance. Bullets pinged all around him. Dust kicked up from his feet as the shots ricocheted off the ground. "I could see shrapnel coming off the wall," he recalled. "Oh, yeah, I thought I was going to die."

Kyle was nearing the breaking point. "I was suckin' wind; my legs were burnin'; I thought I was going to puke. I felt like quitting," he admitted, with a palpable hint of shame. "I felt like stopping and saying, 'Fuck it. You win. You got me.'"

That feeling was hardly new for Kyle. It was one of several times that morning—in the span of just half an hour—that he was sure he was going to die.

Fallujah is an ancient city with a storied past. Seated in central Iraq, it is thirty miles due west of Baghdad, where a highway linking three capitals—Baghdad, Damascus, and Amman—crosses the Euphrates River. It's known as the City of Mosques, as more than two hundred of them dot the metropolitan area.

Although its political and economic significance has fluctuated over time, Fallujah's importance grew dramatically during Saddam Hussein's regime, and it became one of the pillars of the so-called Sunni Triangle. Just two miles from Fallujah is an opulent Baathist resort called Dreamland, where Hussein's monstrous sons, Uday and Qusay, regularly spent time. At its peak during the Hussein regime, Fallujah's population numbered more than four hundred thousand and may have topped six hundred thousand.

It has, in the words of the BBC, "a long history as a rebellious city." In 244 AD, at the Battle of Misiche, the exalted Roman army suffered a great defeat in this vicinity. More recently, the city became a symbol of insurgency against the American-led coalition. The March 31, 2004, attack on four US contractors—in which the charred, mutilated corpses of the ambushed men were hung from a Fallujah bridge—produced one of the most grisly, lasting, and emblematic images of the Iraq war to date.

US forces responded to that incident with an intense, bloody offensive in early April 2004 designed to root out and kill insurgents. That assault, called Operation Vigilant Resolve, lasted for several days. The results were largely mixed. Hundreds of insurgents were reportedly killed in the offensive, but the US military never truly accomplished its mission of eradicating Fallujah's insurgent activity.

On April 9, just five days after the offensive began, the United States called a unilateral cease-fire. Some limited fighting occurred in the weeks that followed, but on May 1, 2004, US forces withdrew from Fallujah and turned over military operations to the Fallujah Brigade, a nascent unit of Iraqi forces. That brigade, however, proved utterly hapless. Within weeks, American military commanders recognized that the Iraqi unit was ineffective in fighting against insurgents. Just five months later, the Fallujah Brigade disbanded and turned over its weapons to the enemy fighters. Fallujah fell back into insurgent hands.

Over the ensuing months, conditions in Fallujah deteriorated and, by late October 2004, the situation became untenable. An estimated two thousand to three thousand committed insurgents were entrenched there, using the city as a base to launch attacks against coalition forces. Jordanian terrorist Abu Musab al-Zarqawi, the gruesome leader of al-Qaeda in Iraq, was thought to be there too. Coalition forces believed that he and other militants were using a network of safe houses strewn throughout the city to hide hostages and videotape heinous beheadings.

Iraqi and coalition officials concluded that they must pacify Fallujah before the upcoming national elections, scheduled for January 2005. The city was a lethally festering sore that could destabilize the approaching vote. An offensive was planned for early November. Leading up to the assault, the American military pummeled the city with "precision strikes," targeting insurgents' safe houses and weapons caches. US forces warned Fallujah residents, through loudspeakers and leaflets, to evacuate. Most did just that: an estimated 80 percent of the city's residents fled before the assault.

On November 7, 2004, more than ten thousand American troops, supported by two thousand Iraqis and some British units, launched the offensive on Fallujah. The US military named it Operation Phantom Fury, but the Iraqi defense minister later renamed it Operation al-Fajr—*fajr* is the Arabic word for "dawn." The objective was to root out insurgents and deny them safe havens in Fallujah. That meant clearing out the sprawling city block by block, street by street, building by building. It was a Herculean task, requiring extensive close-quarters combat against a committed and ruthless enemy.

"The city was a ghost town," Kyle recalled in his unhurried, understated voice, which bore hints of a southern twang but fell short of a drawl. He was perched on the roof of a house in a middle-class neighborhood as part of Operation Phantom Fury, looking out over the sprawl of Fallujah. American and Iraqi forces had begun their furious assault on the city three days earlier. Few Iraqis in this neighborhood had dared to stay. The ones who did remained holed up in their houses. No one was out in the streets. No *people*, that is—dogs were everywhere. Emaciated and friendless, they roamed neighborhoods and rummaged through debris, scrounging for food. Even more ubiquitous was the dust. It covered everything with a layer of pale soot, swirling up from the street as vehicles passed, invading mouths and eyes when the wind whipped through.

The city's streets formed a massive grid, with main avenues crisscrossed at right angles by lesser streets. Narrow alleyways snaked in between the roads, carving narrow corridors in the city's blocks. The overall effect, Kyle recalled, "was extremely structured—how you would expect a civilized city to look." Low-slung buildings—in this neighborhood, mostly houses— lined the streets and alleys. The houses followed a consistent pattern: two or three stories, square, unimaginative in structure. Their colors were uniform, too—some uninspired variation of brown or gray. Most properties had small, barren courtyards featuring tufts of wilting grass, enclosed by tall, foreboding walls made of concrete.

A sniper, Kyle had been paired with another SEAL marksman for an "overwatch" mission. Their job was to protect a Marine platoon as it conducted clearing operations. The platoon, a unit of roughly thirty men from the Third Battalion, Fifth Marines (called the 3-5), was tasked with securing broad sections of the city. As the 3-5 cleared an area—moving down a street, literally from house to house—Kyle and his partner watched for enemy fighters from a rooftop a few houses back and, when necessary, protected the Marines with cover fire.

When the 3-5 made a full sweep down the block, the SEALs would pick their next perch, identifying a tall building in the distance with elevated vantage points, and radio their new site down to the 3-5 Marines. They would then leave the roof, run down the stairs to the street, sprint to the identified building, climb to the roof, and the process would start over again—the Marines would enter the next house, secure it, and then proceed down the block, all under the protection of Kyle's rifle.

This process continued, day after day, until vast areas of the city were cleared. "Those Marines cleared fifty, maybe even one hundred houses like that every day," Kyle said with a heavy dose of respect. It was grueling work, especially because of the searing heat. They baked under the weight of their combat gear. All they could do to alleviate the temperature was roll up their sleeves to the elbow. "We were sweating our asses off. I lost twenty pounds that month."

Three days into the offensive, on the morning of November 10, Kyle and his SEAL partner were engaged in another overwatch mission supporting the 3-5. The designated area that day was a middle-class neighborhood, very different from the pitiable slums that Kyle had seen elsewhere during his deployments. He recalled that the average Iraqi house was somewhat primitive, especially the kitchens. "Some didn't even have piping; they just had buckets that [Iraqis] use to get water to cook." He remembered the counters as particularly rudimentary—"a shelf you'd buy at Home Depot and they'd put a sink in it." The stoves were even worse—"something that your great-grandfather would've had," he recalled. "You were afraid they'd blow up if you turned them on."

But the chosen neighborhood on that day was noticeably more affluent. "The signs of wealth were interesting," he said. "If [residents] had money, they would have chandeliers. Some of the wealthy homes had air conditioners. Not central air, but more than one window unit." American-style toilets, he recalled, were another sign of prosperity. Otherwise, there would be just a hole in the ground.

The 3-5 proceeded through this neighborhood, moving south on a major avenue. It was slow going, as buildings were thickly plotted on either side of the boulevard. But the clearing operations that morning had gone well, with few enemy contacts.

As Kyle ran down the street from one perch to the next, however, he "heard shooting, and wasn't sure what was goin' on." He recognized the sound of the gun instantly: it was an automatic RPK, certainly not "friendlies." He knew immediately that there was a problem. "You know the different sounds of the different weapons," he explained. "The crack that sounds in the air is just a completely different sound."

Kyle couldn't discern where the shooting was coming from, so he scurried up and down the street, trying to locate the shooters. He went up and down the main avenue, ducking in buildings and checking down alleyways. He heard more enemy gunfire. Bullets were whizzing all around. As he made his way around the neighborhood, he saw that two Marines had already gotten hit. He grew increasingly irritated—Americans were getting shot, but no one could figure out where the enemy was hiding.

Kyle was operating alone at this point: his SEAL partner was not only a sniper but also a medic, so he stayed back to treat the wounded Marines. As Kyle turned the corner into an alley, a thick cloud overcame him. He recognized immediately that it was the smoke of a "frag," a fragmentary grenade. The alley was exceptionally narrow—just a few feet wide—and the dust and debris billowed down the passageway toward him. "Black smoke was everywhere," Kyle recalled. He could barely breathe.

Fighting through the haze, he saw that a Marine was lying in the alley, injured by shrapnel. Kyle darted down the passage to help the wounded man, not knowing whether another frag was seconds away from exploding or whether the insurgent who threw the grenade would be lying in wait. He came up on the Marine, grabbed two fistfuls of uniform, and began dragging the man through twenty feet of billowing soot to the main street. There, the Marine medical team took over and hauled the injured man to an awaiting medical Humvee.

Kyle was fuming. The enemy had injured several Marines— the very men he was supposed to protect. He felt powerless. "We just couldn't find the bad guys," he said. It had been ten minutes since he'd first heard the enemy gunfire, and he'd searched the relevant neighborhood, yet still "no one knew where the shots were coming from."

He decided to "circle around and get a different angle." That meant backtracking a few yards, going north on the main street and then east onto another large avenue. A group of Marines stood halfway down the block, clustered near the opening of an alley. Kyle didn't recognize them—they weren't from the 3-5. But that didn't matter: these men said they knew where the enemy was hiding.

The platoon sergeant pointed down the alley and told Kyle that the insurgents were holed up in a stronghold roughly fifty yards down the passage. It was a broad passageway, ten or fifteen yards wide. The ground was paved and the walls were dense, made of stone or cement with stuccolike coating. Dust, of course, covered everything.

Worse, the sergeant said, six Marines were barricaded in a house directly across the alley from the enemy compound, pinned down and taking heavy fire. From Kyle's vantage point, the trapped Marines were down the alley to the left, and the insurgents were across the road to the right. Kyle could see that every time the Marines moved—even if one just peeked out the window—a barrage of gunfire would erupt from the enemy hideout. They were hopelessly trapped. If they tried to escape down the alley, they would get gunned down in a blink of an eye.

The situation was dire, and the SEAL had terrifying visions in his mind: "I saw the Marines getting up and getting mowed down if they moved." He was determined to prevent that from happening. Kyle knew then that he was going to do whatever it took to get those Marines out of that building—even if it meant putting his own life in unimaginable danger. As he later explained, matter-of-factly, without the slightest hint of machismo or self-aggrandizement: "I'd rather die helping those guys out than have a coward's conscience the rest of my life."

It wasn't the first time Kyle had faced such a predicament. In fact, he'd been in a similar situation just a few days earlier, in the opening salvos of the fight for Fallujah. It was during another overwatch mission, with Kyle providing rooftop cover for Marines clearing buildings below. The Marines encountered a group of enemy fighters. A "heavy contact" erupted. The enemy fell back from the street and barricaded themselves into a house. The Marines were left exposed in the street.

After the enemy took cover in the house, Kyle and another SEAL sniper realized they were no longer effective from the rooftop, so they flew down the stairs to the street to support the Marines. By that time, the Marines had barricaded themselves in a building across the street from the insurgents' house. But two of the Marines had been shot, and they lay in the road, writhing in pain.

Seeing the Marines struggling helplessly in the street, Kyle knew what he had to do. "When you see an injured man, you do whatever you can to save him." As a Navy SEAL amongst a group of "young, eighteen-year-old kids" barely out of basic training, Kyle felt he had a special obligation to help these grunts. "It's beaten into your head throughout your training: 'You're the better, more effective warrior.'" That meant he had to go get those Marines, no matter what. And that's exactly what he tried to do.

Kyle and the other SEAL dashed to the men lying in the street, sprinting twenty yards in the open, headlong into a withering torrent of gunfire. Bullets whizzed all around him. He could hear rounds kicking up dirt in every direction. "You can hear the snaps. You know they're close. You just block it out."

He scurried right in front of the enemy's hideout, just a few feet away, to grab one of the injured Marines. The wounded man was screaming, writhing in pain and agony from gunshots to one arm and both legs, and worse, a devastating gut shot that had somehow slid below the Marine's body armor. Despite the volley of bullets filling the air all around them, Kyle began to drag him toward safety.

Kyle saw that he had to pull the wounded man just ten feet to get him into an alleyway, where they would be temporarily safe behind a wall. As he dragged the Marine, Kyle focused solely on the man he was trying to save, doing his best to block out the onslaught of bullets that danced at his feet and zipped by his head. "During the heat of it, you're not thinking about it. You know you could get hit at any moment, and they'll put another belly button in [your] forehead . . . but you just put your head down and go do it."

Kyle tugged and dragged and pulled the wounded man, somehow conveying him over those ten feet until they both fell backwards into the alley. Kyle gave one mighty tug, pulling the writhing, screaming man out of the line of fire. He felt the Marine's blood flowing all over his hands. He heard the man's anguished screams. The Marine pleaded desperately with Kyle, "Don't tell my mom that I died screaming like this!" The screaming continued for a few more agonizing moments. And then it stopped. Years later, Kyle remembered those moments in excruciating detail. "I never met this kid before," Kyle said, "and he wanted me to tell his mother how he died."

Moments like that were etched in Kyle's mind when he was confronted with the trapped Marines a few days later. The last thing he wanted was to have another American die in his arms. "Seeing those guys getting shot up—it would chew me up inside to know that I sat back in relative safety and didn't help them." Kyle recognized that they couldn't get out on their own; he was going to have to get them out. Somehow.

He pulled the platoon sergeant aside and laid out a plan. His idea bore the subtlety of a sledgehammer. Kyle wanted to storm down the alley with a team of six Marines to liberate the barricaded Americans. The remaining Marines would stand at the end of the alley and provide "a barrage of cover fire" from the street. "I wanted them to light up the house," he said. "I didn't care if we actually killed them. I just wanted to keep the [insurgents'] heads down, so we could get those Marines out." As the Marines in the rear laid down suppressive fire, Kyle would lead the six-man team down the alley, open the door of the barricaded house, and provide cover fire as the trapped Marines escaped from their barricade. That meant Kyle and his team would run directly in front of the enemy compound—effectively darting into the middle of a firing range during target practice.

Kyle and the six-man team began to jog down the alley. They clustered along the right wall of the passage, seeking a modicum of safety. Their objective—the barricaded Marines—was fifty yards away.

But the Americans made it only a few steps down the alley. That, Kyle recalled, was "when all hell broke loose."

Suddenly, an insurgent leaped out from the enemy stronghold and leveled a belt-fed machine gun directly at the Americans. Kyle was stunned. "We'd just started out—maybe five yards down the alley. It was like he'd been listening to our plan and he wanted to stop us cold in our tracks before we got ready to execute it." Kyle froze. "It was the initial shock, the disbelief that this guy was doing this. It was a suicide mission for him. And then I realized, 'It's a suicide mission for me, because *he's* got the belt-fed machine gun.'"

It was the first time that morning that Kyle believed he was about to die.

The insurgent started firing the machine gun at the Americans. Bullets pinged past Kyle. The air rushed around him as the shells flew by. Chunks of stucco popped off the alley walls.

In a matter of moments, the insurgent nearly emptied his ammunition belt—some one hundred rounds—before the startled Americans could return fire. Then the Marines "opened up on the guy," Kyle recalled. "He was turned into Swiss cheese." The man's body, punctured with dozens of gaping bullet holes, slumped lifelessly to the ground.

Stunned and dazed, Kyle was standing stock-still in the same spot. He expected to find grotesque, gaping wounds and blood oozing out all over him. "I was rubbing my hand down my body," he recalled, "thinking there was no fuckin' way I didn't get shot."

But he couldn't find any blood, and he couldn't feel any pain. To his eternal surprise, not a single bullet had hit him. In fact, none of the Americans had been hit. The only damage done was to one Marine's pant leg. Kyle would later compare it to a Hollywood western. "It was like a scene out of *Wyatt Earp*, with his duster getting shot up and bullets going through his pants, but he never got hit." The Americans exchanged knowing glances, recognizing that they had literally dodged many bullets. Kyle recalled the general sentiment as "Holy shit! How'd we get away with *that*?"

He looked at the wall of the alley next to him. It had borne the brunt of the attack. He then looked closer, with growing amazement, at the pockmarks. "Anytime a bullet hits that stucco, a piece flakes off, and behind that is a perfectly round bullet hole," Kyle remembered vividly. "It was riddled with holes. For a stretch of ten to fifteen yards wide, it was just bullet hole after bullet hole. It was like walking down a shootin' range and looking at the targets after the guys had been shootin' in the range all day."

Contemplating how he managed to survive seemingly impossible situations, Kyle said, "I have a guardian angel," and added with a wry chuckle, "and he's overworked."

By November 10, 2004, the third day of Operation Phantom Fury, the US-Iraqi coalition had made substantial progress in clearing out Fallujah. American officials estimated that 70 percent of the city was under coalition control, and that more than five hundred insurgents had been killed, along with thirty-eight captured. Media reports noted that numerous insurgent strongholds in and around the city had been destroyed. Iraqi military officials declared that Iraqi troops had discovered several "slaughterhouses," in which insurgents held captives and made grisly videos of their decapitations. Over the three-day ground offensive, eleven American and two Iraqi troops had been killed.

Thinking of those American casualties made Kyle upset. He had no respect for the insurgents. "The only reason they got any Americans is because they would get lucky." They were not soldiers. "They were complete dumbasses," he said with contempt. "Just idiots with guns."

He points to the insurgent with the belt-fed gun as an example. As he thought back about the man—five foot eight, thirtysomething, bearded, close-cropped black hair, and "a good-sized belly"—Kyle's words dripped with disdain. "He should've gotten all of us down." He reflected for a moment before explaining further: "All military rifles are sighted in for three hundred yards. For everyone in the military, three hundred yards is nothing—you should be aimin' and pingin' away at a target. Not just SEAL snipers, but *everyone*. At one hundred yards, guys should be putting two bullets in the same hole."

Then he turned back to the incident in the alley, in which the man shot at the Americans from thirty yards away. "Inside fifty yards is *nothing*. I could do that with a pistol. Not to mention that this guy has a machine gun, which fires one hundred rounds every few seconds. He should have hosed us all down. He may not have killed us all, but he at least should've hit us. If we would have been fighting any military at all—even the Iraqi military—he would have had us dead to rights."

Instead, he was the one who died. And the dogs would eventually get to him. "We called him 'Alpo' after that."

After the scare with Alpo, the Americans scurried back out of the alley to the main avenue and regained their composure. But the other Marines remained trapped in that house, and Kyle wasn't about to back down.

"The plan was still the same. I assumed that we'd try to execute it one more time. So I jumped up and said, 'Let's go!'" He grabbed his rifle and started to sprint down the alley toward the trapped Marines and the enemy safe house.

Over the next few moments, as Kyle put it economically, "things just happened." About halfway down the alley, as he approached Alpo's crumpled body, Kyle realized that he was alone. The Marines hadn't followed him down the alley this time—they were providing suppressive fire from his rear, shooting down the passage toward the enemy compound. It's not clear whether they didn't hear Kyle's rallying cry or whether they opted to sit this round out. What mattered, however, was that Kyle was running down the alley alone. "They definitely made an ass outta me," Kyle recalled with a wry chuckle.

This was rapidly degenerating into a suicide mission. He realized that "there's a good chance I'll get shot the fuck up." But that didn't stop him. Sprinting toward the gauntlet of enemy fire, Kyle thought: "I don't know if this is going to work, but I'm going to go down there and do *something*."

So he did, running down that alley with "guns a-blazin'." But there was another problem: the only gun that Kyle had with him to blaze was a sniper rifle—not exactly the weapon of choice for close-range urban combat. An M4 would have been perfect—"it's light, small, accurate. Its ammunition doesn't weigh as much and its magazine holds thirty rounds." But Kyle didn't have that luxury. He had a semiautomatic 7.62 Stoner Rifle-25, a.k.a. a 762. "It's a big, heavy, long rifle," Kyle explained. A 762 is an extraordinary weapon for long-distance sniping, but not for the task at hand. Worse, the sniper rifle has magazines that hold only twenty rounds, which meant Kyle would have to change magazines quickly.

And that was precisely what happened. Twice. Running right into the teeth of the enemy's fire, Kyle realized his magazine was empty. He had been trained to fire aggressively, "to make yourself seem like a bigger force than you really are. So I was flying through rounds. I went through that first mag pretty damn fast." There he stood, completely alone and totally exposed, right in front of the enemy compound, with no bullets.

"They were shootin' at me the whole time," he recalled. His best guess is that his fire, combined with the suppressive fire from the Marines in the rear, gave him some cover. In the face of the Americans' barrage, the insurgents appeared to duck behind windows and doors. From that defensive crouch, they were shooting wildly, which gave Kyle some time to change out his magazine and continue down the alley toward the trapped Marines.

After a few steps of heavy fire, however, that second magazine was empty. Once again, he stopped, emptied the cartridge, and inserted a new one—all under fire from an enemy just paces away. Kyle's guardian angel was again working overtime.

Kyle finally reached the door of the house that held the barricaded Marines. He knew they had no idea that he was coming, so he was worried that they might think he was an enemy and shoot at him. That meant he had to watch for fire from both sides of the alley. He kicked in the door and shouted with all the strength he could muster, "Get the fuck outta here!"

Kyle crouched just inside the doorframe and provided suppressive fire, shooting relentlessly at the enemy compound as the trapped Marines sprinted out of the house. When the first two individuals dashed through the door, Kyle realized for the first time that the group wasn't all Marines—it also included two civilians: a reporter and a cameraman. The journalists scurried out of the building first and rushed down the alley with their heads down. A handful of Marines started to follow. But they hesitated at the door, apparently unsure whether to run down the alley or join Kyle in shooting at the enemy. Kyle, providing as much suppressive fire as he could with a half-emptied magazine, yelled, "Go! Go! Go!" The Marines needed no more convincing.

As the last Marine flew through the door, he gave Kyle "the last man tap"—the wordless signal that he was the last one leaving the building. Kyle then applied his training: after receiving the tap, he was instructed to look in the opposite direction before moving in a certain path, in order to ensure that he was indeed the last one leaving the location and that his rear was secure. He was going to run north up the alley, which lay to his right. Therefore he first looked left, down the alley to the south. He expected to see a vacant expanse. What was there, however, was something else entirely.

Roughly ten feet away, right in the middle of the alley, lay an injured Marine. To this day, Kyle has no idea how the man got there. No one had been in the alley when Kyle approached the Marines' barricade, and all of the trapped Marines had run out of the house and down the alley to the right.

Yet here lay a man, still alive, in harm's way. He was writhing on the ground, holding his legs in obvious pain. It was clear that he couldn't get up to run to safety.

If what Kyle had done before was incredible, what he did next was closer to superhuman. Of course, Kyle gave a less hyperbolic assessment: "I had to grab my guy and get the hell outta there." And that was exactly what he did.

Standing alone before the enemy compound with little cover fire and no one to attract attention from the enemy guns, Kyle was "the only one getting shot at." He hurried from the house where the Marines were barricaded toward the wounded Marine. Once he reached him, he grabbed the man with his left hand. His right hand held the pistol grip of the sniper rifle, which he'd wedged between his chest and his left arm so that he could continue to shoot at the enemy and give himself a modicum of cover.

In this contorted position, Kyle began to pull the injured Marine back up the alley, toward the safe house more than fifty yards away. That meant crossing back in front of the enemy compound and trying to survive yet another hailstorm of gunfire. Yet again, Kyle's guardian angel was punching the clock.

But then, a sign of hope: Kyle spied a short wall fifteen or twenty yards up the alley. There was only one problem: it was on the other side of the enemy compound. Kyle thought that, if he could just make it to that wall, it would provide enough cover to protect them from the enemy's guns for at least a brief respite. At this point, even a short wall in a dusty alley seemed like an oasis in the desert.

So he made for it, dragging the wounded Marine with his left hand and shooting with his right hand from his improvised, hunched-over position. Kyle scurried down the gauntlet, crossing right in front of the enemy hideout, exchanging shots with the insurgents. He was sure yet again that he would get hit, and he braced himself for the inevitable impact. But somehow both he and his charge made it past the gauntlet of enemy fire unscathed. Kyle enjoyed a fleeting moment in which no one was shooting at him.

Fleeting, indeed: seconds later, things took yet another terrifying turn. Kyle could hear the enemy fighters emerging from their hideout and coming toward the alley. If they entered the alley, they would be right behind Kyle and the injured Marine, an easy shot away. Kyle knew he would have no chance. To make things worse, Kyle's rifle was "dry"—for the third time, the magazine in his 762 was completely empty. He couldn't change it then and there, though, since that would mean he'd have to stop running and let go of the injured man. And that was not an option.

Indeed, there was only one thing to do: sling his rifle on his back, grab the wounded man with both hands, and "haul ass." The insurgents "got off a few rounds," which Kyle could feel flying past him. Chunks of the stucco popped off the walls, exploding in small clouds of debris. Dust kicked up around him as the shots ricocheted off the ground. Yet again, Kyle was sure he was going to get hit.

That was when Kyle neared the breaking point. He was ready to give up. He was prepared to die.

Desperately out of breath, Kyle swallowed back his fatalism. "The inner drive just won't let you give up," he said. Somehow, some way, he just kept running, kept lugging the injured man up the alley, kept dodging as bullets zipped at his head.

Thankfully, the Marines in the safe house were engaged by this point, shooting down the alley at the enemy behind Kyle. For a few nerve-racking seconds, as the insurgents shot up the narrow alley at Kyle and the Marines shot down the passage to provide him cover, Kyle was literally caught in a cross fire. Yet again, Kyle somehow escaped without a scratch.

The Marines' aggressive suppressive fire soon sent the enemy fighters scurrying back to their hideout, giving Kyle enough time to drag the Marine up the rest of the alley and behind the safe house. As he turned the corner behind it, a Humvee was waiting to pick up wounded personnel. Kyle's Marine, who turned out to be a lieutenant, was immediately taken to get treatment for his wounds.

After a day full of life-threatening situations and astonishing heroics, Kyle finally enjoyed a moment of something like real safety. He fell to his hands and knees and ripped off his helmet. He sat there for a moment, trying desperately to catch his breath.

After liberating the barricaded Marines, Kyle recognized that he had completed only half the mission: the insurgents were still alive. There was no way Kyle was vacating the area without "dropping" them: "They'd already killed some Marines, and I just wanted to get 'em." So Kyle huddled the Marines around him and devised a game plan for attacking the enemy compound. After a couple of fits and starts, which included almost getting run over by a massive Marine track vehicle, Kyle led the group on a successful raid of the enemy compound and killed all of the enemy fighters inside.

Kyle's day was just getting started. He didn't get a chance to take a break or ponder what had just happened. He just simply went back to the overwatch assignment for another five to six hours.

Over the next few days, the US-led coalition continued its resolute march through Fallujah. By November 13, it announced that it controlled more than 80 percent of the city. By November 16, nine days after the offensive began, fighting was limited to pockets of insurgent activity.

By the end of that day, the coalition announced that it had secured the city, accomplishing the primary goal of Operation Phantom Fury. Thirty-eight American troops and six Iraqi soldiers died during the operation. An estimated 1,200 insurgents had been killed, with hundreds more captured. Sixty mosques were reportedly damaged in the fighting, and thousands of homes and buildings were destroyed.

For his actions on that day in Fallujah, Petty Officer Chris Kyle received a Bronze Star Medal with Valor Device. In characteristic fashion, he downplayed the importance of the honor: "It's just an award. If I did this for awards, I'd have been outta here a long time ago."

Kyle never learned the names of the reporters or the Marines barricaded in the house, or of the lieutenant that he dragged those harrowing fifty yards up that dusty alley to safety. But he did find out that the injured Marine survived.

Kyle returned to his family after that deployment in October 2008 and retired from the Navy in 2009. Kyle's achievements over the course of his military service are astonishing. With 160 confirmed kills, Kyle was the most lethal sniper in American military history. The US military honored Kyle with a stunning array of commendations: two Silver Star Medals, five Bronze Star Medals with Valor Device, one Navy and Marine Corps Commendation Medal, and two Navy and Marine Corps

Achievement Medals. One of the Silver Stars was awarded for Kyle's actions during a 2006 deployment to Ramadi, an epicenter of al-Qaeda and insurgent activity. According to the citation for that medal, Kyle conducted thirty-two sniper overwatch missions and "personally accounted for ninety-one confirmed enemy fighters killed and dozens more probably killed or wounded." Media accounts reported that insurgents dubbed him the Devil of Ramadi and offered a reward of eighty thousand dollars to anyone who could kill or capture him. Other Navy SEALs reportedly referred to him as the Legend.

Following his military service, Kyle authored *American Sniper: The Autobiography of the Most Lethal Sniper in US Military History*, which stayed on the *New York Times* best-seller list for months. Kyle reportedly donated the proceeds from the book to help other veterans.

He also devoted time to helping veterans in need, such as establishing a nonprofit entity that provides troubled veterans with exercise equipment and counseling and taking veterans struggling with post-traumatic stress to the shooting range to help them cope with the transition to civilian life. Kyle and a friend took one such trip with a Marine veteran on Saturday, February 2, 2013. Tragically, the former Marine shot and killed Kyle and his friend at the shooting range. A police search warrant affidavit stated that the Marine told his sister and brother-in-law immediately after the shooting that "he couldn't trust them so he killed them before they could kill him."

Ryan Welch next to an Apache helicopter prior to a mission near Shindand Air Base, Regional Command West, Afghanistan, in June 2011. Courtesy of Ryan Welch.

Ryan Welch
"My Buddies' Keeper"

By the time he was eight or nine years old, Ryan Welch knew that he wanted to fly helicopters. He was always obsessed with war games as a kid. GI Joe and *Star Wars* were particular favorites. "I was game for basically anything that had a gun or involved shooting," Welch recalled. "My sister called me a warmonger as a kid."

Welch credits his upbringing for the passion for all things military. His father, whom Welch calls his hero, was a career Army officer, which meant Welch grew up on military bases around the world. But more importantly, Welch said, he grew up in a hunting family, and so he was around guns all the time. "I have just always liked to shoot. It's built into my DNA."

Welch had a special reverence for helicopters. He recalled the moment when his fascination began. His father was stationed at Fort Bragg and took him to a live-fire exercise. Young Ryan watched the exercise as the soldiers shot guns and cannons down the range. "Pretty cool," Welch recalled. But the coolest display for the young kid was the Cobra helicopters. They flew overhead and decimated a few unlucky targets at the far end of the range. That sealed the deal. "I just looked at my dad and said: 'I'm going to do that when I grow up.'" His father responded with a pat on the head and said he could do whatever he wanted.

From then on, Welch fixated on helicopters. "I always knew I wanted to fly armed helicopters and never looked back."

His fixation would soon find a specific target. In the early 1980s, the Army introduced the Apache as the new generation of attack helicopters. They were fast, sleek, and amazingly powerful. They were, in Welch's words, "the workhorse of attack helicopters." Soon after the Apaches came on the scene, the youngster received a life-changing gift: a calendar full of Apache pictures. "I thought that was the coolest thing ever." He was blown away by the Apache's futuristic look and its incredible technology—particularly the fact that the aircraft's guns were aimed by sensors linked to the pilot's helmet. Plus, Welch explained, the Soviets were America's enemy at the time, and tanks were their strong suit. The Apache was designed to be a tank-killing machine that would equalize the battlefield dynamics, which made it that much more attractive.

While Welch's obsession with Apaches began in grade school, another life-changing focus would develop during his college years. When considering his post–high school options, Welch knew he wanted to follow his father's lead and pursue a military career. So he focused on military schools and ultimately chose to attend America's oldest private military college, Norwich University in Vermont.

Welch's years at Norwich instilled deep-seated values about "the brotherhood of arms." From their first day at Norwich, cadets are taught about the unyielding bond between fellow soldiers. "As cadets," Welch explained, "you go through hardships in your freshman year, and the only way through them is to bind together and never leave a buddy behind." Those values were cultivated through rigorous drills that teach cadets to conform their behavior for the benefit of the team. "Everyone has to march the same way. Everyone has to dress the same way," Welch recalled. "And there was a price to pay if you didn't. There were many, many push-ups—many, many nights up polishing brass and polishing boots because if there is one guy who looked screwed up, *everybody* was screwed up."

Eventually, Welch said, the "draconian conformity" taught cadets that individualism does not work. Instead, they developed a sense of responsibility for each other and a desire for their fellow soldiers to succeed. They learned that "no one out there is a superhero. No one has clairvoyance. No one is bulletproof. It takes people watching your back constantly to be successful." In short, they learned that they were their buddies' keepers.

Those values would guide Welch on a daring rescue mission on a dark night in 2004, deep in hostile territory known as the Triangle of Death.

Welch graduated from Norwich University in 1997 and immediately went to flight school. For the next two years, he trained with various helicopters and learned basic combat techniques. When it came time to specialize in a single aircraft, Welch requested the Apache. ("Of course," he said sheepishly.) He had done well in flight school, so his request was granted. Welch was thrilled that he would realize his dream of becoming an Apache pilot: "When you talk to an Army aviator, they will love whatever aircraft they fly—but in my opinion, everybody secretly wants to fly the Apache."

Over the next seven years, Welch would learn the intricacies of his beloved aircraft. He marveled at its awesome power and cutting-edge technology. He mastered the helicopter's night-vision flying systems, which include an intricate mix of night-vision goggles, infrared sensors, and unaided eyesight. The infrared system links the aircraft's weapons systems to the pilot's right eye. "It's a pretty neat system," Welch said, describing how his helmet display unit projects an infrared image in front of his right eye so that he can essentially see through the helicopter and view his entire surroundings. "Imagine putting your head on the front of the helicopter and looking out the front—that's basically what it's like. There is really no obstruction of the pilot's view—you can look through your feet and see the ground." As a result of this targeting system, Apache pilots can find targets in an unparalleled manner. "If we can see them, we can shoot them. There are not a lot of places they can hide."

Welch grew to appreciate the Apache's unique impact on the battlefield. "As far as assisting the ground commanders and ground troops, it is a one-of-a-kind aircraft. It has the ability to change the tide of the battle." Welch described how the mere appearance of an Apache in a firefight can result in victory: "When you show up on station, it can go from a complete hair-ball to complete calm in a matter of minutes because the enemy knows you can knock his house down, so they choose not to fight anymore usually." Then he added, beaming like the child at the Fort Bragg live-fire exhibition all those years ago: "It's pretty awesome to have that power at your disposal."

After graduating from flight school in 1999, Welch served in South Korea and at Fort Campbell, Kentucky. In March 2002, soon after the commencement of combat operations, his unit was called up for deployment to Afghanistan. It would be his first combat tour, and Welch recalled that the actual deployment was not exactly smooth.

His unit had been on alert for potential deployment several times before, and the alerts had always ended up as false starts, so no one expected that they would actually be deployed anytime soon. On one Saturday morning, his supervisor called and told them that they were going to Afghanistan. "We all chuckled," Welch recalled, "because we'd all heard that before." The next day, however, Welch was making a TV dinner when he received a phone call notifying him that he would in fact be deployed and that his plane was leaving in roughly forty-five minutes. He was forbidden from telling anyone. His wife was out of town on an extended business trip, so Welch had to run around his house unplugging the appliances, closing windows, and locking doors. He yanked his TV dinner out of the oven and wolfed it down on the way to the plane. The time between his flight to his arrival in a combat zone was roughly sixty-six hours. "Crazy days," Welch remembered.

Soon after arrival in Afghanistan, Welch and a colleague were dispatched to Bagram Airfield north of Kabul. As his flight descended toward the landing strip at Bagram, the Air Force crew strapped on their Kevlar gear and instructed Welch and his colleague to get out of the plane immediately upon landing, out of fear for enemy fire. "We're not sticking around," they were told. Welch and his partner hopped out of the plane upon landing and scooted off the runway to a grassy area to get out of the way. It was dark, and the two men stood cluelessly in the grass, not knowing where to go or whether anyone was even around to help them. As they watched the plane on the tarmac, they spotted a man approaching them, waving a flashlight and yelling frantically. They could not hear the man because the jet's engines drowned everything out. Then, they looked down at the grassy area around them. "That's when we realized they were standing in the middle of a minefield." Welch looked back on the incident, which he described as "a little nerve-racking," with a smile. "We'd been in Afghanistan all of eighteen hours and almost blew ourselves up. That was a little bit of a religious experience."

But there was one more hiccup in Welch's deployment. A few weeks after he arrived in Afghanistan, a friend checked on Welch's house back home, just to make sure everything was in good condition. The friend reported that Welch's house was incredibly hot—because the oven was on. Evidently, Welch had forgotten to turn off the oven after snatching his TV dinner before his flight, and the appliance had been on, roasting his house, for about a month.

Although his travel to Afghanistan was eventful, his time there was relatively quiet for a combat pilot. He returned home after roughly six months and deployed to Iraq in 2004. Welch saw his first real combat there, during missions in support of the 2-5 Cavalry "Lancers," First Cavalry Division, operating in Sadr City, a sprawling and impoverished suburb of Baghdad that was the home of the insurgent Mahdi Army. He recalled the sensation of taking fire from enemy forces on the ground as he bobbed and weaved in the air, dodging the streams of light coming from tracer rounds. "It was pretty hairy," Welch said. "[The insurgents] had some heavy-caliber machine guns and they weren't afraid to use them. Fortunately for us, they weren't very good shots."

He recalled the first time he was responsible for the death of insurgent guerrillas. He was in an Apache, providing protection for a convoy doing work on the south side of the city. The cavalry team started receiving mortar fire from an insurgent mortar team. The ground unit spotted the insurgent personnel and radioed Welch the coordinates for the enemy position. Welch and his copilot began to maneuver their Apache to target and engage the enemy mortar team. Then, before Welch had fired a single shot, the American team on the ground reported on the radio: "The Apache just took out the mortar team." Welch responded with surprise, because they had not even located the insurgent team at that point, much less taken any action against them. He asked in less than diplomatic terms: "What are you talking about?" It turned out that, in their maneuvering to the proper location, Welch and his copilot had flown over the top of a Sadr City building—directly above the insurgent mortar team. The powerful gusts from the Apache's propeller swept (or scared) the insurgents off the roof, and the American ground units watched the men fall from the building. Flying above, Welch looked down and saw the insurgents lying dead on the street below. They were Welch's first confirmed kills. "And we didn't even fire a shot," he said.

Welch found combat exhilarating. "For a young guy, I was so charged up to be in the fights that you forget that between those glowing tracers there are three or four other bullets," he said. "When you're flying through it, you're thinking: 'That's kinda cool.' There is separation when you are in the air—you can't really hear all the gunfire and you don't have the time to get scared . . . until you get back and you realize you have holes in your blades or a popped tire and you realize one of those bullets could have hit you in the head." Still, he enjoyed a high after flying successful missions and likened the experience to scoring a touchdown in a football game. After returning from a battle, Welch said, "there are high fives and everyone's got a story to tell and you relive it over and over again. The camaraderie is great between the aviators and the ground troops. I guess that's why I like it so much."

Combat also heightened his enthusiasm for the Apache even further. He spoke passionately about the relationship between ground troops and aviators, evoking the principles of brotherhood and mutual responsibility instilled at Norwich, and how the Apache is instrumental in protecting the ground units. "The bond between the air guys and the ground guys is pretty thick, pretty strong," Welch said. "The Army aviators like to think of themselves as an extension of the ground guys. We're not removed—we live with the grunts. We have to fly through all the bullets that are getting shot at them. So I guess the bond—the responsibility to keep the ground guys protected—is a pretty meaty one."

And that is why he loves the Apache—because it is un-paralleled at protecting the ground troops. "You can sense the change in emotion from the ground guys when the Apaches arrive on a battle scene. That's why I love it so much—to see the look on the soldiers' faces when we're able to get them out of a bad situation or come to their aid when they need us," he said with evident pride. "You can hear them cheering on the radio. If they're pinned down, you can hear the sense of relief in their voices when you're able to scare the enemy away or take care of them. It's so rewarding. That's what it's all about."

On the night of October 16, 2004, Welch was piloting his Apache on a routine mission over the Tigris River outside Baghdad, reconnoitering sites that insurgents had previously used to launch mortars and rockets into the Green Zone. About fifteen minutes into their mission, another pilot issued a curious call over the radio. The call struck Welch as odd, particularly because it came over the "guard" frequency, the military's emergency radio frequency. The other pilot stated that two helicopters had crashed and that two pilots had been killed and two survived, but he was confused about the site of the incident. When the pilot reported the call sign of the downed helicopters, Welch knew it immediately—it was the call sign of his battalion's sister unit, and he knew a number of the pilots in that battalion.

Worse, Welch knew the zone in which the helicopters had reportedly crashed—it was southwest of the Baghdad airport in a dangerous, insurgent-infested area that was frequently called the Triangle of Death. Welch was a bit leery of going headlong into such hostile territory. He and his copilot had no idea what the situation on the ground was, other than the fact that enemy fighters were usually all over the place and there were no friendly ground forces anywhere nearby. Worse, an Army helicopter had recently been shot down there, killing two of Welch's close friends.

They flew in anyway. Welch and his copilot headed straight for the zone to look for the crash site and the surviving pilots. Welch engaged the infrared-vision equipment to look for heat emanating from the crash or the surviving pilots. He flew over one location that had a significant fire, but Iraqis regularly burned their household trash, so this blaze looked like any of the numerous fires raging in and around Baghdad at that time. To get a closer look, Welch's copilot, who was flying the plane as Welch manned the guns, flew the aircraft over the site. They were highly concerned that the other helicopters had been shot down and that they were essentially flying right into an ambush, so they moved fast and low to the ground.

As they flew over the site, Welch saw a ring of fire with what seemed like boards lying across the top—they still were not sure it was the crash site. Only when the surviving pilots said over the radio that the Apache had just flown overhead did they realize that the blaze was coming from the downed helicopters.

Welch quickly realized that a ground convoy and even a medevac helicopter would take too long to get to the site. He understood that he and his copilot would have to rescue the downed pilots. And that meant landing their helicopter in hostile territory.

Welch asked the survivors over the radio how they were marked, so he could see where they were. They responded that they had put out their strobe light—the emergency light that every pilot has, which has a filter that makes it visible with night-vision goggles but not infrared sensors or the naked eye. But Welch had lent his night-vision equipment to a colleague earlier that night and had only infrared gear, so he couldn't see the strobe. He asked the pilots to take off the filter so that the strobe light was just a naked bright light that Welch could see from the Apache. It was a risky move, as it would also make the light visible to the enemy forces who might be lurking in the darkness.

The downed pilots took off the strobe's cover, and the Apache pilots quickly spotted them, about ten to fifteen feet down in a deep trench near the crash site. Welch's copilot surveyed their surroundings and found a suitable landing site roughly three hundred feet to the south of the crash site and the survivors' position. They could not set down closer, Welch explained, because landing the aircraft requires a large, flat, open field, and the men were situated in a deep ditch.

The copilot brought the helicopter down, kicking up a huge amount of dust and large clusters of tumbleweeds into the air. It was a delicate moment. Welch hoped that the men would race over to the helicopter, so they could get out of there right away. Every second that the Apache was on the ground was highly uncomfortable for Welch, because being on the ground is the Apache's most vulnerable point. "We're a fifty-foot-long helicopter, so we're sitting there like a school bus," he explained. "Any guy in the bushes with an AK-47 or an RPG can probably ruin your day." They were basically a huge sitting duck.

But nothing was happening. Welch recalled a long, uncomfortable pause filled with eerie silence. Finally, Welch said intently over the radio: "Ok—we're ready—*come on over.*" Then one of the downed pilots responded that the other was severely injured and could not move. They were still in the ditch one hundred yards away and needed help.

When he heard that, Welch's initial response was "Aw, *shit.*" He knew what it meant: he would have to get out of the helicopter, cross three hundred feet of hostile territory, and carry the injured men to the helicopter.

Welch discussed the situation with his copilot for about five to ten seconds—they both understood what had to happen. They could not simply take off and land closer to the injured men. Welch explained that they were essentially committed to their landing spot once the helicopter touches ground because of "brownout," which is the disorienting wall of dust and debris kicked up by the helicopter's rotor system. The brownout causes pilots to lose sight of the ground through all of the dust, making it impossible to take off and land nearby. So the aircraft was staying put, and one of them had to go get the survivors.

Welch understood that he was the one who had to get out of the aircraft—he was the mission commander, and he believed it was his responsibility. Also, his copilot was in the rear seat that night, meaning that he was responsible for flying the helicopter, while Welch operated the guns from the front seat. Given the hostile nature of the territory and the possibility of enemy fire, the helicopter might have to take off at any moment, and Welch wanted the rear-seat pilot to remain in the helicopter to allow for a quick escape.

"Looks like I gotta get out and get these guys," Welch said to his copilot. As he unclipped himself from his seat and prepared to depart the helicopter, Welch said to his copilot, "If you start taking fire, just leave." He knew that meant he would be stranded in the Triangle of Death with two injured crash survivors, but he figured that getting the Apache destroyed or disabled on the ground would be a worst-case scenario—then they would be stranded *and* without any air support.

Welch then hopped out of Apache and jumped into the maelstrom of dust swirling around the helicopter. He did not carry much gear with him. Most of the gear was standard survival equipment for Army pilots: a survival vest that held a radio, strobe light, first-aid kit, knife, compass, navigation gear, and a GPS. He also carried a pistol, a rifle, and a few additional rounds of ammunition. He had "enough to shoot myself out of a bad situation, but not a whole lot of offensive capability." Welch recalled that all of the gear was flapping around in the wind and must have made for a comical sight. "I was a big mess. I had cords hanging off of me. It was not the picture of grace that I thought it would be."

Wasting no time, Welch started running away from the helicopter toward the crash site, the length of a football field away. As he ran through the field, it was completely dark—a "zero-illume night" in military parlance. There was no ambient light at all, except for fire coming from the burning helicopters one hundred yards in the distance. And Welch had no night-vision gear. He was running furiously, stumbling blindly through the uneven field, tripping over clumps of claylike muck and large tumbleweeds of hard, fibrous plants that dotted the terrain. There were also large trenches and ditches that appeared intermittently. "I fell down a big ditch just before I got to those guys—picked myself back up and dusted off," Welch said with a self-deprecating chuckle. "The night-vision goggles definitely would have helped."

As he scurried through the field, Welch quickly realized just how far away the survivors were. "Everything looks closer in the air," Welch said. But he kept moving forward.

As he neared the crash site, he could hear the popping and whistling sounds and mini-explosions coming from the wreckage—the noise of the fire consuming the downed aircraft and the ammunition in the crashed helicopters igniting in the blaze. He knew the bodies of the two killed pilots lay in the wreckage and briefly considered trying to collect their remains. He knew one of them from a previous assignment. "He was a good guy," Welch recalled with a somber tone. But, with the fire still active and the ammunition "cooking off" so violently, it was just too dangerous to go near the wreck. "I felt horrible," Welch said of not retrieving his colleagues' bodies, but there was no way he could get them. "It was completely engulfed in fire."

So he ran directly to the survivors' position. Seeing them for the first time startled Welch because both men were bleeding profusely out of their eye sockets. He figured that the pilots' night-vision goggles must have smashed into their faces during the crash. One pilot was more injured and was obviously delirious. "He got his bell rung pretty good," Welch said. "He had a vacant look on his face." He was also waving his weapon around aimlessly, so Welch quickly swiped it from him, saying: "I'll take that." The man could walk, but his steps were slow and labored. "It was like an old man shuffling along," Welch said. So Welch and the less wounded survivor propped up the injured pilot with his arms draped over their shoulders, and they began hobbling back toward the helicopter.

It was an excruciating experience. "The thing that sticks out in my mind was that it was *really* slow going getting back to the helicopter," Welch recalled. They were exposed in the middle of an open field in hostile territory—the Triangle of Death, no less—and they were near a very loud helicopter. He knew their window of escape could slam shut at any moment. An anxious voice pounded in his head, saying: "We've gotta go! We've gotta go! We've gotta go!"

Welch implored the men to hurry up, but they could go only so fast due to their injuries and mental state. Worse, the men had various cords and gear tangled all over their bodies, which impeded their movement. After a few minutes of trudging across the field, Welch's heart sank. He saw that the survivors' strobe light—blinking brightly in the darkness—was dragging behind one of the pilots, attached by a cord. It followed only a few feet behind them as they crossed the open field, identifying for everyone precisely where they were. Welch promptly took out his survival knife, cut the cord, and chucked the light as far away as possible.

Then they resumed their belabored procession to the helicopter. As they plodded through the field between the violent, windy, noisy environment around the helicopter on one end and the crackling mini-explosions of the crash wreckage on the other, the atmosphere became disconcerting to Welch. "It was almost an eerie kind of peace," he recalled. So Welch implored the men to hurry up. "I was trying to urge them to move faster because I didn't want to get shot."

Welch was exhausted and sweating profusely at this point. But adrenaline was powering him forward. Eventually, the men made it back to the helicopter. "It seemed like we were gone forever," Welch recalled.

But they were not out of the woods yet.

As they approached the helicopter, Welch was trying to figure out how he could get the men to safety. The big problem was that only two people could fit inside the Apache. The helicopter has no bay area or storage, as in a larger aircraft. Every space is filled with either fuel or ammunition, so there was no obvious place to put the survivors. Welch initially expected that he and his copilot would sit inside to fly the helicopter, while the surviving pilots would sit on the outside of the helicopter, using a technique called self-extraction.

Self-extraction is a risky procedure used to evacuate people from dangerous situations. It is usually used as a last resort. Welch explained that the Apache has two avionics bays running down the outside of the helicopter, and during a self-extraction, the rescued person sits on one of the bays on the outside of the aircraft and attaches himself behind the helicopter's back canopy using a carabiner and an extraction strap. Then the rescued person sits outside of the aircraft as it flies away.

Welch emphasized that the technique is hardly sophisticated: "It's not cosmic, by any stretch," he said. "There is no special technique." But, despite its simplicity, sitting on the outside of a helicopter as it flies through the air at one hundred miles per hour is perilous. In fact, although the military practices every other technique and maneuver ad nauseam, the self-extraction technique is simply too risky for normal training.

But self-extraction did not seem possible in this situation because at least one of the survivors seemed too injured and too deeply in shock for such a task. Welch thought to himself: "I'm not going to be able to get this guy to hold on to the outside of the helicopter." So he made an instinctive decision: he would put the man in his seat and he would strap himself to the outside of the aircraft.

With that, Welch yelled in the man's ear: "I'm going to put you in my seat. Don't touch anything!" Then he began hoisting the man into the front seat of the Apache. Once again, the scene was not a model of gracefulness, Welch explained, as the Apache sits four to five feet off the ground. Welch had to heave the man up to his shoulders and over the edge of the aircraft. "So here I am," Welch depicted the moment with self-deprecation, "squatting this guy up over [the lip of the helicopter] to get him in the aircraft and then shoehorn him into the front seat." Welch did not know the extent of the man's injuries or whether his hoisting him into the aircraft and jamming him in the seat would cause him further injury, but that was secondary in Welch's mind—he believed that putting him in the cockpit was the only way to evacuate him safely, and that was the only thing that mattered at that point. "I would never forgive myself if they'd gotten shot or kidnapped while waiting for someone else to show up."

Welch finally wedged him in, hopped up on the side of the helicopter, and reiterated sternly in the dazed man's ear: "*Do.*

Not. Touch. Anything." The injured man looked back at Welch with a semivacant look and nodded in apparent assent. Welch threw the canopy door closed and prepared to help the second pilot attach himself to the outside of the aircraft. Welch knew the man was less injured than the first, so he figured securing him to the helicopter would be easier.

He was wrong.

As he turned toward the man, Welch saw that he was walking away—back toward the crash site. Welch was starting to get antsy, as their window of opportunity to escape without attracting enemy fire seemed to be dwindling rapidly. He yelled down to the man that he needed to get up on the side of the aircraft. The pilot hollered back that his commander was back in the wreckage, and he did not want to leave him. "You gotta leave, man," Welch pleaded, trying to convey the sense of urgency. "Your commander doesn't want you *dead.*" The man continued to protest, saying that he did not have his extraction carabiner. Welch climbed up on the Apache and asked his copilot for his carabiner pack and gave it to the other pilot, but the pilot still insisted on staying with his commander. Welch was quite frustrated at this point, certain that the delay would create major problems for them. "I had to get aggressive with him," Welch recalled. He told the man: "You gotta leave! Your commander would want you to leave. I can't wait for you." The man reluctantly got up on the shelf on the side of the helicopter. As he clipped the man in with the borrowed carabiner, he glanced inside the aircraft—his copilot was watching him intently from the backseat and whirled his finger around, giving him the universal "Hurry up!" signal. Welch finally secured the reluctant man to the side of the helicopter and leaped to the ground.

He darted around the back of the helicopter and climbed up on its left side. He took out his carabiner and clipped to the helicopter's back canopy. Secured to the aircraft, he banged on the roof and squatted down, bringing his face to the side of the window and gave his copilot the thumbs-up. Then he sat on the avionics bay running on the outside of the aircraft, with his feet resting on the missile launcher. "I never thought in a million years that I'd actually do it," Welch said of the self-extraction technique. "But when it came time to do so, it was second nature."

And they took off, with Welch and the less injured survivor riding on the sides of the aircraft. At first, Welch felt relatively secure, despite the intense wind coming from the rotor above. "I never felt like I would fall off." In fact, Welch planned on providing some security during the flight, thinking that he could watch for enemy forces and shoot his rifle if a problem arose. "As we started taking off, I had my rifle out and I was ready to return fire." But, as they ascended and sped up, "I quickly realized that was not going to be that effective."

The wind coming from the rotors grew progressively more intense as the copilot increased the speed. Worse, Welch's helmet was channeling the airflow right into his face. "It was pretty violent," he said, comparing the impact of the wind to continuously wiping out on water skis or riding a speeding motorcycle without a helmet. He could not shut his mouth or keep his eyes open because the wind was blasting him so hard. All Welch could do was duck his head down, putting his chin to his chest, and grasp the extraction strap as tightly as possible.

As he clung to the strap and took the punishment from the incessant wind, the situation finally sunk into Welch's mind. And he started *laughing*. He was not sure why, but thinking about what he was doing—flying on the outside of an Apache in the middle of the Triangle of Death—made him chuckle to himself incredulously. He thought to himself: "I can't believe I'm doing this. What the hell have I gotten myself into?!" "It just struck me as funny," he said.

Funny or not, he still wanted get on terra firma as soon as possible. "That flight could not have been short enough for me." As they peeled away, Welch caught a brief glimpse of a convoy of ground troops coming down the road to secure the crash site and recover the remains of the deceased pilots.

Welch's copilot took them to a nearby forward operating base with a hospital, which sat more than twenty kilometers (twelve to thirteen miles) away. The flight took roughly ten minutes. Welch praised his copilot for flying the aircraft so well in such difficult circumstances without a second pilot. "It's a two-pilot helicopter," Welch explained. As they slowed down for the descent, the wind let up. "I was pretty glad when we were on our approach," Welch recalled. "It was a huge relief to get there."

As they landed, Welch was concerned about the injured pilot in the front seat of the helicopter. He unbuckled his extraction strap and hopped off the helicopter to the tarmac. He ran straight to the hospital to get a litter to carry the injured men.

The hospital staff asked what medevac unit Welch flew for. "I'm not a medevac pilot," Welch responded, to their surprise. "I'm an Apache pilot."

Once the hospital staff had the situation under control, Welch hopped back in the helicopter, and they headed back to their camp. During the flight home, his copilot said he wanted a cigarette. "I don't smoke," Welch said, "but it sure sounds like a good idea." Welch did not know how long the rescue operation lasted, but the total time from the original takeoff to time they landed back at their camp was no more than an hour. "I call it a really crazy hour," he said.

For their efforts to rescue the downed pilots that evening, Welch and his copilot were awarded Distinguished Flying Crosses, the fourth-highest combat award. Receiving an award was not something Welch ever expected or even thought about. So he described receiving a commendation as significant as the Distinguished Flying Cross as "kind of surreal," because he had heard of other pilots receiving the commendation, but many of them had died during their missions.

Welch was modest about his Distinguished Flying Cross commendation. "It's not something that I advertise that I received. In the Army, you're only as good as your next mission. So I don't think about it too much," he said. "I'll be okay if I never get a higher award."

He was also self-effacing about his actions during the rescue, saying: "I think anybody else would have done the same thing as we did, given the opportunity." He credited his training and his belief in the principles of brotherhood, instilled from his very first days at Norwich through his tenure in the Army. "It's a cliché to say, but your training kicks in in a high-stress situation and your values and your training are the things that will carry the day," he said. "Those values were ingrained into me in school, and throughout my military career to that point."

Despite the harrowing moments of the rescue, Welch said: "I wouldn't trade it for anything. I was glad I was able to help and be there. We didn't have to kill anyone and we helped someone out. It was a good story. It came at a good time, when the American people were looking for some good news to come out of Iraq."

The big thing, in Welch's mind, was that the two pilots survived. "I'm just glad those guys are okay," he said. Welch never saw the two men after the night of the rescue. The day after the episode, Welch's copilot saw the men having lunch at the mess hall and spoke with them for a while. He reported that they were banged up pretty badly, but seemed to be in decent spirits. But Welch never saw them again. "It is kind of an oddity, I guess, but we never really ran into each other." Welch was okay with that, however, saying: "We don't look for thanks or anything like that. You just kind of move on." Although he never interacted with the men, the wife of one of the survivors later tracked Welch down and e-mailed him the following message: "I just wanted to thank you for taking care of my husband [and his copilot]. Having a loved one get hurt (or worse) over there is something we wives pray never happens. But, I am comforted by the fact that you are doing your best to look out for each other . . . There really aren't enough words to express my gratitude, but again, thank you."

Kyle Need on Masirah Island off the coast of Oman in May 2010.
Courtesy of Kyle Need.

Kyle Need
Midnight Rescue in
the Middle of the Ocean

Kyle Need loved the water. Growing up in Virginia Beach, Virginia, he was into all kinds of water sports—surfing at the beach, swimming at the pool, whatever, as long as it involved water. So, in 2004, when he was nineteen years old and searching for something meaningful to do with his life, Need decided to be a rescue swimmer for the US Navy. He originally wanted to enlist with the Coast Guard, but his father—who had retired the previous year as a Navy medical officer—influenced him to join the Navy instead.

Need knew it was the right move for him. He had tried college after high school, but he quickly realized that it wasn't for him at that time. Then he worked construction, although he spent most of his time partying with friends. After about a year of "doing whatever I wanted to do," Need decided that he wanted a change for the better. He longed to do something substantive, and so he went to talk to the local Navy recruiter. Kyle didn't need a hard sell; within twenty minutes of his first meeting with the recruiter, he decided to enlist and knew that he wanted to be a rescue swimmer—it seemed like a perfect combination for him: pass the minimum physical requirements test and he would be able to jump out of helicopters and swim all day.

He could not have been more wrong.

In late 2004, Need started the battery of training programs required to be a rescue swimmer. It started with boot camp and went through a slew of other programs, like "learn to fly in a helicopter" school, as Kyle called it. The training regimen eventually culminated in the Rescue Swimmer School, one of the toughest schools in Navy training. Going through that gauntlet was a major wake-up call for the hard-partying surfer boy. "I went into my job-selection process completely ignorant of what was required of me to become a rescue swimmer," he recalled. "I had to buckle down and pretty much get it together."

Once he finished all the programs, he finally became a rescue swimmer and was assigned to Helicopter Antisubmarine Squadron Five, known as HS-5. The squadron's core search-and-rescue mission was called overwater SAR, which meant rescuing people stranded at sea, particularly American aviators whose planes had crashed in open water. But HS-5 was responsible for far more than just overwater SAR, like conducting search-and-rescue missions on land and in combat, resupplying seaborne Navy vessels, working with special operations teams on naval special warfare missions, and leading antisubmarine warfare operations. With their expansive portfolio of responsibilities, Need's outfit trained extensively. "Our day-to-day job was to train and be ready," Need said. "We did much more training than we actually did our job."

For their overwater SAR training, they practiced every permutation of water rescue imaginable. The general contours of a water rescue were somewhat straightforward: the four-man team was supposed to board their helicopter, with the pilot and copilot in front and the crew chief and rescue swimmer in the back, and depart from the aircraft carrier to the search area. After locating the survivors, the pilots would engage the automatic approach mechanism on the helicopter to hover the craft either directly above them or nearby. The rescue swimmer was supposed to jump in the water or would be lowered down on a thick two-hundred-foot steel cable with the helicopter's hoist.

The rescue swimmer would then swim to the survivors, check them for injuries, and get them connected to the helicopter's cable with one of a variety of apparatuses. The crew chief would then operate the hoist to lift the survivors to the helicopter. The rescue swimmer would usually go up with the last survivor.

But, Need cautioned, generalizing rescue missions would be a mistake. "No two rescues are alike," he said. "Every one is completely different and has different factors." For safer situations, like a daytime operation in which the sea state is stable and weather is good, the rescue swimmer will jump from the helicopter directly into the water. Jumping in is faster than getting lowered down on the cable by the hoist, Need explained, and those precious moments could be critical. "The survivor could be facedown or in some type of trouble, so we need to enter the water ASAP to assess the survivor." For those jumps, the pilots hover the helicopter at ten or fifteen feet above the sea in order to place the swimmer as close to the survivor as possible so the swimmer does not have to waste energy getting to the survivors. "When you do a rescue, even if you only have to swim twenty feet," Need said, "you put out every ounce of energy you have since your adrenaline is pumping."

Once in the water, the swimmer will signal to the crew chief that he landed safely, swim to the survivor, and assess the situation. If the survivor is not injured, the swimmer will connect him or her to the helicopter's cable through the survivor's harness or with a rescue strop, which is a large floatable sling placed under the person's arms. When a survivor is injured, the swimmer may use a rescue litter, which is a backboard that will stabilize the injury, or a rescue basket. The swimmer's job, Need explained, is "to prepare a survivor as quickly as possible and get them up in the helicopter where we can provide treatment."

When the circumstances are trickier—like a rescue at night, in a rough sea state, or with oil, fire, or debris on the water near the survivor—the rescue operation changes dramatically. In those situations, the helicopter will hover much higher—seventy feet above the water—and, rather than jumping into potentially dangerous waters, the swimmer will be lowered down with the cable. Once in the water, the swimmer will unhook from the cable and then swim to the survivors to complete the operation.

For the most precarious scenarios—in Need's words, "big seas and situations where you just want to get in and out no matter what the injury of the survivor is"—the crew will use a technique called direct deployment. In those rare operations, the helicopter will hover forty feet above the sea, and the swimmer will be lowered down by the cable directly on top of the survivors. Instead of disconnecting from the cable and swimming to the survivors, the swimmer will stay connected to the helicopter throughout the operation. Also, the regular rescue equipment, like the basket and litter, may be too time consuming and cumbersome for such turbulent scenarios, so the swimmer will use a thin sling called a quick strop to connect the survivor to the cable. As its name suggests, the quick strop is designed for speed—for hooking up the survivor to the cable and getting him or her in the helicopter as fast as possible, no matter what.

The unit practiced the whole spectrum of operations— ten- and fifteen-foot daytime jumps, seventy-foot hovers, and even forty-foot direct deployments—over and over. Need even practiced the most basic part of his job—putting on his rescue gear—"a million times." He understood that when the call came, it would be an emergency, and he would have to throw on his equipment fast. He didn't want to waste precious moments fumbling around with his equipment while an American pilot was clinging to life in a raft out at sea. So he practiced until he could put on his entire outfit—a dry suit, rescue harness, mask, fins, booties, and hood—in less than two minutes.

The one type of training they did not do that often was open-water rescues at night. They had some nighttime exercises, but they occurred in a pool—quite different from the dynamic elements found in open water. Other training at night is generally in a local river or another calm body of water. "It would be too dangerous for us to actually go out into the open ocean and put someone in the water to conduct training without it being necessary," Need explained. "There are just too many things that can go wrong in that environment." That lack of nighttime open-water training did not bother Need. "If you do enough training and go through situations in training about what to expect," he said, "it's enough to prepare yourself for it."

That confidence and training would be tested on the first night of their deployment in January 2010.

On January 2, 2010, HS-5 deployed on the USS *Eisenhower*, a massive nuclear-powered aircraft carrier that Kyle equated to a small city. Like its namesake, the vessel is affectionately known as "Ike." The *Ike* left that night for its deployment in support of Operation Enduring Freedom in Afghanistan, which would take them east through the Atlantic and the Mediterranean to the Gulf of Oman.

The weather on the first night of their deployment was simply awful. "It was the middle of the winter," Need recalled, "and we were in one of the worst snow/ice storms that I had ever heard of." Commander F. Byron Ogden, the executive officer of HS-5, remembered the conditions as "horrific," with "snow, sleet, hail, and winds gusting to fifty knots." Incredibly, the sea state was so rough that the waves were tossing around the gigantic *Eisenhower*. "If you can imagine how big ocean swells need to be to rock an aircraft carrier," Need said, "then you can understand how we felt as we were rocking around in the open ocean."

Around 7:30 that night, the men learned that a sailing vessel with one man onboard was in distress between 250 and 300 miles off the coast of South Carolina. The Coast Guard was far closer to the endangered boat—the *Eisenhower* was more than 230 miles away at the time—and therefore they would handle the rescue.

Nonetheless, Need's four-man team was a backup plan, so they prepared for the mission with a briefing just in case. Despite the turbulent conditions, Need wasn't terribly concerned about the situation, as they had briefed for many previous operations that never panned out, and it seemed like the Coast Guard had everything under control. "I knew we had to be ready for anything, but I thought there was little to no chance we would head out on that mission." So, after the briefing, Kyle headed back to their office on the ship to hang out and watch a movie.

Around 9:40 that night, roughly two hours after the initial distressed-vessel report, the team learned that the Coast Guard helicopters were experiencing maintenance problems and that the *Ike* might be called upon to execute the rescue. In light of the extreme weather conditions, the rear admiral commanding the entire carrier strike force asked Commander Ogden whether his crew could execute the mission and how long it would take to get airborne. Ogden replied that they could most definitely complete the mission successfully and safely and that their helicopter could be airborne in thirty minutes. The rear admiral then gave the order to launch.

After getting the call, the four-man team—Ogden, copilot Scott Pichette, crew chief David Brandon, and Need—raced to get ready for the mission. Need was still in the unit's office, relaxing and watching the movie, when the call came in. He popped up and sprinted through the ship's passageways to the flight equipment room.

He struggled in the cramped space to put on his gear—a buddy had to toss equipment to him as he threw everything on in a flash. His extensive practice in putting on his regular dry suit was helpful, but only to a point. The weather was so bad—so cold and dangerous—that the regular gear would not suffice. "With a dry suit, you are only as warm as what you have on underneath," Kyle explained. "The suit keeps you dry, but your body temperature will decline rapidly if you aren't properly dressed." He knew that the flights to and from the scene would be long and frigid, not to mention the fact that he would be plunging into the freezing water to rescue the survivor, so he would be exposed to bitter temperatures for an extended time. Plus, he had always been trained to dress for a flight as if the helicopter were going to crash, not for comfort during the ride.

So he layered up like never before, donning a long-sleeved T-shirt, long-john Polartec fleece pants, a long-sleeved Polartec shirt, a thick fleece jacket, and two pairs of long socks. Then he stretched and tugged and pulled his dry suit over all those layers. "You can imagine how much my movement was constricted," he recalled later. He checked his gear three different times to make sure he was prepared. While he normally could throw on his gear in less than two minutes, it took him between five and ten minutes that night. "Putting it all on sucked," Need said, "because I only had a few minutes to get up on the flight deck and help out with starting up the helicopter." So once he triple-checked everything, the overstuffed rescue swimmer hurried up to the flight deck.

As Need was overdosing on fleece and Polartec, the aircraft carrier had changed its bearing and was speeding as fast as possible toward the last known location of the survivor. Even though they were hurtling forward at thirty-plus knots, the crew actually felt a wind at their backs—the storm's winds gusted at forty to forty-five knots from the ship's rear (the stern) toward the front (the bow), in the opposite direction of the carrier. "The resultant effect on the flight deck," Ogden explained, "made it like you were standing in winds of ten to fifteen knots." The helicopter, however, could not launch in such a strong tailwind, and the *Ike* could not go fast enough to overcome the storm's gusts.

The only viable option was to turn the helicopter around and launch into the wind, facing the ship's stern. Ogden explained that this maneuver is affectionately known as "launching Chinese." At 10:42 that night, more than three hours after the first report about the vessel came in, the helicopter launched Chinese into the raging storm. That would be the easiest part of their mission.

*   *   *

The storm, Need recalled, was "the worst weather that I had ever been outside in—not just flown in. We were getting beat around pretty good." Even Commander Ogden, a seasoned helicopter pilot with more than 3,500 hours of flight time, called the flight a "harrowing" and "dramatic" experience: "That night was, without a doubt, the most severe weather I had ever experienced while flying my helicopter." But the four men in the helicopter were pros, and the roller-coaster ride, while distracting, did not rattle them. "Everyone in the aircraft had enough experience to not get sick in those situations," Need said later, "so it didn't affect the way we felt." In fact, the storm helped the rescue effort by providing a powerful, fifty-knot tailwind that propelled the men toward the search area.

Shortly after the helicopter left the *Eisenhower*, the team established contact with the Coast Guard aircraft on the scene. They reported bad weather in the rescue area—snow, sleet, and hail—and that they were not able to see the sailing vessel at all. They could locate two rafts, but could not see whether anyone was in them. They informed the Navy team that the search area—the last known location of the survivor—was 178 miles away. That meant the HS-5 team would be flying in the storm at least an hour.

"An hour flight is good in some ways, but horrible in others," Need said later. The crew prepared everything before the mission, and Need wasn't really responsible for doing anything during the flight—"I was just there to go in the water," he said—so he had a lot of time to think about the rescue. It also gave the team time to talk about what to expect and how they were going to handle any situation that could pop up.

But the downtime also had disadvantages. "It also allowed me to concentrate on the fact that if something went wrong, I could end up getting left in the freezing water with twenty-five-plus-foot seas three hundred miles from civilization," he recalled. "I wish I could say that I was excited and calm but I was a little worried."

Need's defense mechanisms kicked in to fight the instinctive focus on negative outcomes, largely by ignoring them: "In those situations, adrenaline is your best friend and takes over so you don't have to concentrate as much on the possible consequences. You run all the bad things that could go wrong in your head but then try not to think about it." Beyond blocking out what could happen, he turned his attention to the procedures he would employ and "exactly what I needed to do to get back safely and not kill anyone."

The other three men in the helicopter also helped him cut through the potential nightmare scenarios stalking around in his mind. They were trained professionals, after all, and they used a tried-and-true method of confidence building: they made fun of him. Ruthlessly. "Luckily," Need said, "I was in this situation with three good guys who were all very professional, but also knew me well enough to make fun of me and give me grief the entire flight out to keep me laughing. Actually, the last thing my crew chief Dave said to me before I took my helmet off to get in the water was 'You better not fuck this away, Kyle!'"

Despite his copious training over the previous five years, Need had been on only one rescue mission before that night. The circumstances surrounding that operation were the polar opposite. "It was around 1:00 p.m., sunny, and seventy-five degrees out, with the water chilly, but nothing crazy," Need recalled. The aircraft carrier's planes were launching for training exercises, and Need's team conducted a "plane guard mission" in which they flew close to the carrier in case something bad happened with one of the jets in the training exercises.

During the practice runs, an F18's jet wash blew a seaman off of the carrier's flight deck and into the water. Need's team got the call. They rescued the man and had him back on deck within minutes. Need would later describe the operation as "very textbook."

Need could only hope that the rescue mission on January 2, 2010, would be so successful.

* * *

The Coast Guard aircraft at the scene that night—a massive C-130—could not execute a rescue operation itself, so it guided the Navy helicopter throughout the hour-long flight toward the survivor's last known location. When they arrived, crew chief Brandon used night-vision goggles to scan the water for the raft and the survivor. In a mission like this, Need said, the most painstaking and time-consuming part of the mission is usually locating the survivor. The stormy conditions did not help. "We had 0 percent illumination that night, with snowy skies and no moonlight," Need recalled. Their only help was a rescue light mounted to the bottom of their helicopter, but it was no match for the stormy conditions.

Nevertheless, almost immediately after they arrived at the search area, the crew chief spotted the survivor on a raft in the water. "*Damn*—that was fast," Need thought to himself. Brandon told the team that the survivor was waving his arms and a flashlight around like crazy.

It happened so quickly that the pilots tried to put the aircraft into position for the pickup right away. But getting the helicopter into position and hovering in the same place would prove particularly difficult that night. After Brandon spotted the survivor, Ogden took the helo down from its flight altitude of three hundred feet to two hundred feet, and Pichette attempted to engage the helicopter's automatic approach system. In a normal nighttime situation, the pilots would engage the automatic approach system to fly the helicopter to the desired hover altitude and then maintain a stable hover over the water, which would facilitate the rescue operation.

But the ocean's thirty-foot waves were too much for the computer to handle. Ogden recalled seeing the tumult from two hundred feet in the air, saying: "The swells were so great that the survivor was going in and out of view from less than one thousand feet away." As a result, the automatic approach would not engage. Ogden did not want to waste time by circling back around, so he decided to conduct a manual approach and hover the helicopter at eighty feet above the survivor.

Ogden brought the aircraft down to an altitude of eighty feet, and Pichette attempted to engage the helicopter's automatic hover system. The computer failed to attain a stable hover for roughly thirty seconds before it finally engaged. "That," Ogden said later, "turned out to be a bad idea." The computer was trying to keep a consistent height above the water, but tracking the tumultuous waves meant throwing the aircraft up and down fifty feet at a clip, like a schizophrenic elevator. As the computer plunged the aircraft down toward the water, Ogden wrestled with the manual controls to keep it from getting too close to the water.

After a couple iterations of soaring up and plummeting back down, Ogden had had enough. He decided to disengage the automatic controls and fly the helicopter completely by hand. It would be a particularly difficult maneuver in particularly difficult conditions, but Ogden was able to stabilize the helicopter enough to deploy Need down into the water. Even when Pichette was able to engage the helo's other computer system as a backup, Ogden stayed in manual control, recalling later: "I wasn't in a trusting mood just yet."

He maneuvered the helicopter into position, and the team prepared for Need's descent into the water. Given the darkness and the extreme conditions in the water, this was no time for jumping in. Instead, the team would employ the direct deployment technique, the worst-case process in which Need would be lowered down by the helicopter's hoist and remain attached to the massive steel cable throughout the operation.

Sitting in the back of the helicopter and preparing to go in the water, Need was oblivious to their fifty-foot fluctuations. He sensed that the hover was rough, but it was so dark that he couldn't see anything—the survivor, the raft, or the thirty-foot swells. "When it is that dark, you have no relative sense of direction or altitude," Need explained. "If you can't see a stationary object outside the aircraft, then you can't feel how much the aircraft is moving around. As long as it didn't knock me down, I probably wouldn't know if we crashed or not until I was thrown around the cabin and my face was wet."

Need was hooked on to the cable with his rescue harness and was ready to descend into the water. He approached the door and peered out into the darkness.

The scene, he said, was surreal.

"It was really, really dark," Need recalled. "It was the darkest night I had ever seen. No moon, no stars, no ambient city light, just our aircraft rescue light and snow reflecting that dim light." He couldn't see much, but he could discern the ocean's swells coming up toward the aircraft. It was the first time he'd really looked out and appreciated the conditions.

Need was a bit anxious about the tumult below, but he didn't have time to dwell on what could go wrong—he had a job to do, and someone's life might be at stake. So he dealt with his nerves by focusing on the task at hand. "I remember just thinking: 'All right, do your job and a few minutes from now, you'll be back in the helo flying home to safety. It will only be painful for a bit.'" He had faith in his training and confidence in his abilities—he never thought that he couldn't do the job. He also knew this was a great opportunity, one that he wanted to seize. "You know what you get into when you sign up for this job. You definitely always want to be that guy who made the big rescue, not the guy who couldn't control his emotions and do his job."

And the burst of energy flowing through his veins didn't hurt. "Adrenaline," he said later, "is a great thing."

As the cable lowered him down toward the water, the snow and sleet caked up on his mask and stung his face. "It didn't feel great going down that night," he recalled. The wind was freezing cold, but he didn't notice it pushing him around very much. He knew that his crew chief was "working his ass off to pay out enough slack in the cable to keep me from being tugged around when swells would drop me down and raise me up."

He dangled in the frigid air for a while, but he was in the ocean within two minutes. The water was stunningly cold. "When I hit the water, I was pissed off because I wanted to land in a raft, not forty-degree water." That was the original plan— Need would be lowered directly into the survivor's raft—but due to the problems with the helicopter's automatic approach systems and the heavy seas, such precision was impossible. As a result, crew chief Brandon had to lower him into the water as close to the raft as possible, which was about fifteen to twenty yards away. Need knew that hoisting is not easy in calm seas— much less in a storm like that—but he was still irritated. Swimming that distance in ice-cold, tumultuous water would be painful, and he had hoped the drop would be significantly closer to the raft. So, as the freezing water enveloped his body, he looked up at the crew chief and thought sarcastically: "Really?! This far away?! Thanks, man."

Need wanted to get out of the water as soon as humanly possible. "Looking up and seeing the walls of ocean heading at my face wasn't fun to see." His hands went numb right away, despite his thick, neoprene gloves, and he knew it was not going to get any better. The ocean's swells were picking him up and plunging him down every few seconds, and he understood that the only way to remain oriented was to concentrate on his task and block out everything else.

He scanned the water for the raft and caught a quick glimpse before a wave blocked his view. He darted off in that direction. "I swam as hard as I could," Need recalled, "and realized that I needed to calm down or I was going to waste all my energy."

Need arrived at the raft within a few seconds. The survivor looked at Need and yelled at the top of his lungs, "Man, it's good to see you guys!" Need couldn't really see the man, as he was wearing a huge antiexposure suit with hood. The survivor started chatting with Need, explaining the situation and that he'd been out there for a while and hadn't seen another human for a few days. But Need wasn't interested in small talk. "I didn't have any Hollywood phrases like 'I'm your rescue swimmer and I'm here to help,'" Need recalled. "I just wanted to get my feet on the ship as soon as I could." So he hollered at the man to shut up and jump in the water. Need later admitted that he'd laced "a few expletives in there." The survivor responded with a prompt "Okay!" and jumped in the water.

Need held the man in his arms as they tossed about in the water, trying to hook him into the quick-rescue sling attached to the cable. But the task—which he had practiced countless times—was exceptionally difficult under these circumstances. The recurring surges of water made it almost impossible to breathe, his hands were numb, his arms were occupied holding the man above water level, and he couldn't really see. He struggled with the sling for a minute, and eventually hooked it up. He checked the sling three to four times to make sure it was on properly.

Then Need gave the signal to crew chief Brandon to lift them up. The hoist quickly picked up the slack in the line, and the cable grew taut. As the slack disappeared, Need recalled, the cable dragged the men in the water and then "the sea just dropped out from under us and we got yanked pretty hard through the air." The men in the helicopter worked hard to avoid getting the men hit by a wall of water—Brandon timed the hoist with the peak of a surge, and Ogden added power to the helicopter to take the aircraft up another thirty feet, which pulled the men out of the water by the time the next swell rolled through. The men dangled in the air, spinning around rapidly, as the hoist pulled them seventy feet to the helicopter. "It hurt pretty badly," Need said, noting that it was probably even worse for the survivor because the quick-rescue strop is "not built for comfort." Worse, the weather had grown even more severe, with a thicker wall of snow and sleet rolling in and pounding the area. As they sliced through the punishing storm, Need prayed that the hoist would hold and not jam up.

The cable held and the men eventually got up to the helicopter. Need and Brandon shared a triumphant high five. This part of the rescue operation—from the moment Need left the helicopter to the time he was pulled back into the cabin—lasted less than six minutes. "The efficient execution of this most demanding evolution in conditions that go beyond defining 'extreme weather' was so incredible," Commander Ogden said later, "that I cannot find the words to adequately express the achievement."

Although the water rescue had been remarkably successful, the HS-5 team knew the mission was not quite done. They had to assess the survivor's condition and treat any injuries, not to mention fly back through the storm to the *Eisenhower*. The weather had deteriorated even further and, more importantly, the fifty-knot tailwind that had propelled them on the way to the search area was now a brutal headwind, so their pace slowed dramatically as Ogden and Pichette navigated through the storm. "My pilots worked their butts off," Need recalled, "dodging sleet and snowstorms, not wanting to climb in altitude so we could avoid freezing conditions."

In the helo's cabin, Brandon and Need checked the survivor, who was slightly hypothermic, but otherwise seemed to be to be alert, uninjured, and in reasonably good health. Need recognized that the man was also in a mild state of shock when he told them that he was not hungry or thirsty. So they wrapped him in blankets and tried to keep him conscious with meaningless banter and a barrage of snacks and water.

On the flight back, the man told the crew that monstrous waves had caused catastrophic damage to his sailboat and eventually sunk it. He had a raft, but it had drifted away from him as he abandoned the boat. He was wearing a personal flotation device and appropriate survival gear, so he swam after the raft. He tried desperately to catch it, but after ten to fifteen minutes, he became exhausted and gave up. He told the crew that he thought he was going to die. As he was tossed in the swells, another raft miraculously drifted into him—it was a device that a Coast Guard plane had dropped blindly into the search area. He climbed into the raft and waited. When he saw the Navy helo, he became ecstatic and started waving his light up in the air at the aircraft, hoping to catch their eye. Ogden recalled that the survivor said it was a miracle that they had found him, and that he was only alive today because of their efforts. "He definitely found God," Ogden said.

The flight back to the *Eisenhower* took nearly twice as long as the flight out to the search area—about an hour and a half. After they landed, Need walked the survivor downstairs and handed him off to medical personnel. Need then changed out of his rescue gear and grabbed some dinner with his crew.

Although the team had just pulled off an incredible rescue and literally saved a civilian's life, there was no welcoming crew or hoopla of any sort. It was nearly 2:00 a.m. and most of the sailors, including all of Need's friends and coworkers, were sleeping. The only acknowledgment of their efforts was a literal pat on the back from their squadron's commanding officer. "This isn't *Top Gun*," Need explained, "where you shoot down one or two aircraft and the flight deck is flooded with people celebrating your return and carrying you on their shoulders."

Despite the businesslike reception on the *Eisenhower* that night, the Navy later honored Need with a Navy–Marine Corps Medal, the Navy's second-highest medal for heroism in non-combat situations. Receiving such an illustrious award was a "pure surprise" for Need. Pichette had told him on the night of the rescue that he was nominating him for a medal, but Need had no idea it would be that distinguished. "I felt that no matter what happens down the road, I can at least be proud of that award and that night."

Looking back on the rescue, Need readily deflected credit to his teammates. He characterized crew chief Brandon's work on the cable as "amazing" and credits his skill on the hoist with saving his life and the survivor's as well. "It could have been a lot worse," he said. Need praised Pichette's "flawless" handling of the radio communications and mission-essential aircraft equipment, saying: "That type of mission could not happen without a guy like Lieutenant Commander Pichette handling the situation the way he did. Not too many pilots could handle the amount of pressure that he did that night, but he had the experience to back it up." Need also lauded Ogden's ability to navigate through the storm. "It shows how much [of] a damn good pilot Commander Ogden is."

Ogden likewise focused on the unit's collective effort: "It was a tremendous team effort that I am very proud to have been a contributing member." He used glowing language in discussing Brandon's performance on the hoist, saying: "The required level of precision by the hoist operator [Brandon] cannot be overstated in this situation. If the cable isn't positioned correctly when the swimmer and survivor are being hoisted up out of the water, serious damage can be done to either or both individuals. Brandon remained calm, cool, and collected, while expeditiously providing me clear, concise commands to fly the aircraft to the best position to hoist the swimmer and survivor out of the water safely." Ogden lauded his copilot's efforts as well, saying: "LCDR Scott Pichette was also outstanding in the performance of his duties. It was great to have an experienced pilot sitting next to me—not a brand-new 'nugget'—as this rescue required the best efforts from a highly seasoned and extremely skilled crew. I am extremely thankful that I definitely had the A team on that rescue!"

But Ogden reserved special praise for Need, whom he called "the true hero" of the rescue. "He is the one," Ogden said, "that selflessly put himself in harm's way to save another man's life."

Dan Foster in Yusufiyah, Iraq, in November 2007.
Courtesy of Dan Foster.

Dan Foster
Walking a Step Higher

In the early morning hours of May 21, 2010, Dan Foster was *really* bored. The Army specialist was pulling guard duty in a tower watching over a remote outpost in Afghanistan. It was seven and a half hours into an eight-hour shift, and Foster was ready to get out of the damn tower.

The tower was a drab concrete structure standing about sixteen feet off the ground, with a tiny circular room at the top. The room was roughly four feet across with concrete walls about six inches thick. The walls rose to the middle of Foster's torso and continued again above his head, creating an open-air window. The opening wrapped around the circumference of the structure, which allowed a guard to view the entire landscape around him.

Inside, the room was spartan. Sandbags filled the area, limiting a guard's movement and making the small space even more claustrophobic. The most important feature of the room was the large machine gun that was propped on a tripod and pointing menacingly out the window toward the entrance of the base, fifteen meters below. The machine gun, called a Mark 48, was a serious weapon. It was belt-fed, capable of releasing about two hundred rounds per minute, and Foster felt confident in shooting accurately at targets up to 1,800 meters away (more than a mile, or just less than twenty football fields laid end to end).

"You could fuck some things up with it," Foster said matter-of-factly.

Beyond the Mark 48 and the sandbags, the room was bare. There was no furniture, save a few empty bottles and a trash bag. The bottles stood ready in case the guard had to relieve himself. The trash bag was necessary for bodily functions that the bottles could not handle. Leaving the tower to hit the bathroom was not really an option. "The last thing you wanted to do," Foster explained, "was to call for somebody to take part of your shift." So the bottles served as a guard's makeshift toilet.

Foster did not mind that. In fact, going in a bottle provided a nice break in the interminable monotony of tower duty. "It was almost a game for us—we carried as much water as we could up there and [left] like five to six liters of piss bottles up there," Foster said. "Pissing takes time away. Sittin' there filling up a bottle, it's almost a like a checkpoint you're getting to."

That, Foster explained, illustrates how boring guard duty in the tower could be: *urinating in a bottle* was an eagerly anticipated highlight. Each shift, which lasted between eight and twelve hours, was like being stranded on a deserted island. Not only was a guard alone in a cramped room, but the atmosphere was like a sensory deprivation chamber. Next to the tower sat the base's power generator, which emitted a loud hum that drowned out most other noises. There was not much to see either, despite the open-air windows. "We were surrounded by houses with high, built-up walls around them, blocking most of the view behind them," Foster said, "and behind them was just a wall of mountains, behind more mountains." Worse, Foster frequently worked from 10:00 p.m. to 6:00 a.m., when the darkness surrounding the base was simply impenetrable.

Working in the tower was, therefore, all about "killin' time." Guys would go nuts up there, Foster said, stuck in "that little four-foot circular room with no contact at all, day after day after day."

Foster combated the boredom by planning his thoughts before he went on duty. "I would come up with a list of things I was going to think about that night. I'd set time limits on them," he said. Up in the tower later that night, he would try to stick to his schedule. "I'd sit there [thinking about the issue] and forty-five minutes or an hour later, I'd look up and say, 'It's time to think about this topic now,' and switch over and start thinking about something else."

His designated topics ranged from the solemn and profound to the coarse and frivolous. He thought about his buddies in other bases who were experiencing brutal combat. He developed a "master plan" for his post-Army life, which seemed to change with every shift. Girlfriends were a forbidden topic: "Thinking about a girl back home with eight to ten lonely hours of guard duty—it's a worse tease than being at a strip club." In his lighter moments, he pondered his next workout schedule and read articles that his father sent about his beloved Los Angeles Angels. He also spent considerable time imagining ideas for tattoos and ranking his favorite flavors of oatmeal. (Maple and brown sugar, "a trusted staple," easily beat out blueberry and apple cinnamon.)

It was so quiet because there was nothing to do—as in no threats to guard against. They were in the middle of nowhere. Few cars or trucks ever entered their base, so watching over the front gate for insurgent vehicles coming up their dirt path usually meant watching for nothing. Foster estimated that he worked in the tower for one thousand hours up to that night and had experienced only one minor contact with enemy forces—and they turned out to be innocent civilians, a mistake for which Foster was severely upbraided by his commanders.

So, as he sat in the tower at 5:30 in the morning on May 21, 2010, Foster was looking forward to ending his daily torture. He and the other two guys on the guard team, stationed at the base's entrance on ground level, had already called for the next group of guards, and they were just waiting out the shift.

This particular stint was a tad better than normal because Foster had snuck his iPod up to the tower. It was a breach of Army rules, which forbade any interference with a guard's hearing, but he did it anyway. "It would keep me sharp and alert," he insisted. Still, out of deference to the rules, he compromised by taking out one of the headphones. An Akon song blared away in his right ear. He didn't really like hip-hop and R & B like Akon—punk and jazz were more his speed—but one of the other guys had downloaded it to his iPod during their deployment to Iraq a year earlier, and Foster never bothered to delete it.

As the clock inched toward 6:00 a.m., Foster watched the sun rise and the scene brighten with ambient light. Although sunrise was undoubtedly welcome—it was beautiful and also meant the end of his shift—it was a precarious time. The changing light during those transition periods, sunrise and sundown alike, made it difficult for eyes to adjust. So, Foster understood, they were the key times that insurgents attacked. He had seen dozens of uneventful sunrises in the tower, though, so he was not terribly concerned. Foster mostly thought about the epic nap he would be taking in just a few minutes.

That was when he heard the pop . . . pop . . . pop . . . pop of gunfire near the base's entrance.

Growing up in Costa Mesa, California, Dan Foster knew from a young age that he was going to enlist in the Army. At first blush, Foster might not have been a traditional recruit. He had virtually no military pedigree—only his grandfather served for a "short but honorable" stint before being discharged for polio—and none of his friends showed the slightest interest in going down that path. In fact, Foster said, most of his friends were "indies and musicians"—hardly typical Army candidates. He too was "a huge band nerd," mastering the trombone, saxophone, drums, and piano in his teens.

But the youngster had been enchanted by the military in middle school. "What got me," he recalled, "was sitting at home and watching the History Channel." The old World War II documentaries captivated the young teenager, particularly the soldiers' tales of adventure and their sense of accomplishment. "The stories the guys were coming back with—all of them seemed like they had done something with their lives, and they walked around a step higher. I wanted to come back with the stories that these guys were telling." The History Channel, he said only half jokingly, is the most effective recruiting tool for the Army.

He also credited Stephen Ambrose's books for sparking his interest in the military. *Band of Brothers*, in particular, was "one of the biggest things that set me off." He devoured the book, amazed by Easy Company's perseverance through countless struggles. The image of the men suffering through the awful snowstorm in the Ardennes Forest during the Battle of the Bulge moved him. "The stories of the guys freezing their asses off in a forest—the shittiest situation you can imagine yourself being in—for some reason that sounded like . . . a good idea for me to do," he said with a laugh. Reading those stories, the youngster thought to himself: "That sounds fun! I want to be able to say, 'I did that!'"

So on the morning of his seventeenth birthday in October 2005, the first day that he was eligible, Foster enlisted in the Army. At the time, conditions in Iraq and Afghanistan were quite grim, and he understood that he would deploy to a combat zone. "That part didn't spook me much," he said. In fact, that was the whole point—he chose the infantry so he could figuratively freeze his ass off in a forest somewhere, like his boyhood heroes in Easy Company. "It seemed like a good idea," he said with a chuckle. There was absolutely no uncertainty in Foster's mind—this was the right thing to do.

Foster had just started his senior year of high school when he enlisted, so he would have to wait until after graduation in June 2006 to go to basic training. After graduation from basic training in October 2006, Foster was stationed with the Third Brigade of the 101st Airborne at Fort Campbell, roughly an hour outside Nashville. His unit had recently returned from deployment to Iraq, so they had a relatively light workload. In fact, when he walked into the unit's bunk for the first time, it was midafternoon and the first thing he saw was a noncommissioned officer "drunk off his ass." The rest of the unit was already off duty. "What the fuck?!" the new private muttered to himself. "It's 2:00 in the afternoon. Everyone's drunk and only has to work until 2:00? The Army is gonna be *awesome!*"

Foster's first impression of his unit turned out to be somewhat accurate. It was a rowdy bunch of guys, and beer was a constant companion. Problems arose frequently, especially when they encountered guys from other units. "Every third word," Foster recalled, "had to do with how much better our unit was." Those were fighting words in the testosterone-driven environment of the US Army. Their entire combat brigade (around five thousand to six thousand soldiers) were such troublemakers and instigated so many fights that they were banned from Fort Campbell's on-base bar. "About a quarter of the base," Foster said with evident pride, "was not allowed in the bar." Foster recalled one particular night on which someone pulled the fire alarm at the bar (before they were banned), and the drunken throng simply moved the party outside. When a couple of police cars showed up to quell the commotion, the military police were met with a hail of beer bottles. "They just drove away," Foster said with a mischievous smirk.

Despite their buffoonery, Foster's unit did work hard. The training at Fort Campbell, he recalled, was more physically draining than boot camp. They prided themselves on being "violent and aggressive" in combat drills.

In late summer 2007, just under a year after he arrived at Fort Campbell, Foster's unit left for a fourteen-month deployment to Iraq. Their base was near a town called Yusufiyah, which sat on the Euphrates River about twenty miles southwest of Baghdad. It was part of the so-called Triangle of Death, an insurgent-filled area marred by brutal guerrilla attacks and grotesque mutilations and beheadings. "That," Foster said, "was a shitty area." The unit knew the history of the region and prepared for intense engagement. "We went out there ready to kick ass and pound terrorists," he recalled. "The Great Battle was imminent—that's what we all thought."

But they would be sorely disappointed. Their deployment, Foster said, was "*really* quiet." The American surge was in full effect at the time, which basically eliminated the fighting. "Everything completely stopped," Foster said. "No rockets, nothing." In fact, over their fourteen-month deployment in the erstwhile Triangle of Death, Foster's unit gained virtually no combat experience whatsoever.

The lack of action took a heavy toll on the aggressive infantry unit. Although they were happy to return home at the end of their deployment in October 2008, most were disheartened by their experience. "A lot of people didn't reenlist because of what happened [during] the first [deployment]. We didn't want to go sit in another country for fourteen to fifteen months and not do a fucking thing."

The inaction stung Foster particularly hard. He had joined the Army to see action and gain a sense of accomplishment. "I was pretty crushed coming back. It felt like I hadn't done *anything*." It was a far cry from the stories he heard on the History Channel.

Back at Fort Campbell, the unit learned it would deploy to Afghanistan in January 2010, roughly fourteen months later. Their destination was a patrol base just north of the Helmand province on the Pakistan border. The region was infested with Taliban guerrillas. When Foster's platoon discussed their destination with units that had previously deployed there, the response was dispiriting at best. "Everybody's reply was gloom, like 'Oh, I'm *sorry*,'" Foster said. "Everybody felt bad for us."

But, after the frustration of the Iraq deployment, Foster and his buddies were excited. They were virtually guaranteed combat experience. "[The insurgents] said they would die before they gave [the region] to us, so we were ready for a fight," Foster said. "Everyone was gung ho about it."

When they arrived in Afghanistan in early 2010, however, Foster's unit was disappointed once again. His platoon, a group of twenty-three soldiers along with a handful of support personnel, was split from its company and assigned to a small police-training station near the Pakistan border. Although the rest of the company was located twenty miles away and another NATO base housing a battalion of US Army personnel was also based within a few miles, their little training post was a relative backwater—certainly not in the hotbed of guerrilla activity that they had eagerly anticipated. "We had a pretty cozy area," Foster said. "All of us were livid—we thought we should be with the rest of the company."

Their mission was to train approximately fifty Afghan soldiers who were responsible for patrolling the border and stopping guerrillas from infiltrating the country from Pakistan. It was the first American-style training those Afghan troops had ever experienced, and the process did not go smoothly. "We were doing what we could," Foster said. "We would go on patrols with them. We had [Afghan soldiers] quit midpatrol—they'd just drop all of their gear on the ground and walk away," he recalled incredulously. "There wasn't a lot of trust between us."

The unit quickly grew frustrated at their middling success with the Afghan trainees. But mostly the unit bristled at the utter lack of action. For the first four months of their deployment, they did not have a single contact with insurgents. In fact, Foster had only one live-fire incident in the first four months—and it was a complete debacle. A team from the unit was patrolling the area, with Foster manning the fifty-caliber gun in the turret of the lead truck. During their patrol, an unknown car rushed toward the convoy. Foster believed it was an insurgent vehicle trying to assault their truck, so he shot a few rounds into the car, trying to stop it before it hit them. It quickly became clear, however, that the occupants were unarmed civilians. Thankfully, Foster's rounds sailed harmlessly through the windshield and injured no one. But Foster was severely reprimanded by his superiors for shooting at civilians. There was, he recalled, "a lot of screaming." (His buddies also tormented him for missing the intended targets. "People were giving me all kinds of shit for putting [fifty-caliber] rounds through the window and not killing anyone.") Those ten seconds were Foster's only "combat" in more than eighteen months of deployment in Iraq or Afghanistan.

They mostly sat around on guard duty, enduring endless shifts at the base's two security posts. Their training station was situated near a significant road, which in Afghanistan meant that it was paved. Vehicles seeking to enter the base had to turn off the main road and drive down a forty-meter dirt driveway to reach the base's sole entrance, which was little more than a chain-link fence.

There was a large dip at the junction of the main road and the dirt driveway, a ditch that had eroded over time. The Army left the trench in place, like a reverse speed bump that required vehicles to slow down as they turned into the base. The driveway was also designed in a serpentine configuration, curving around a few times so that enemy vehicles could not build up steam and rush the main gate. Massive barriers, called Hescos, were placed in the driveway's curves, forcing oncoming vehicles to slow down and follow the driveway. Hescos were huge containers made of a tough, fibrous material mounted onto a chain-link grate, which was then shaped into a box. "You could stand up in the middle of an empty one and put your hands out," Foster said, "and you would barely touch the sides." They filled them with tons of sand, debris, and rubble. "Fill 'em up with sand," Foster said, "and they'll stop anything." Just in case an enemy vehicle navigated through the obstacle-course driveway and arrived at the entrance unimpeded, the unit placed a large truck immediately behind the gate, to ensure that only authorized vehicles could enter.

Two thick concrete security walls surrounded the base. In between were the base's two security posts—the gate and the tower. Three men typically worked on each guard shift—two on the ground level at the gate and one poor soul in the tower. On the ground, the two men inspected incoming vehicles and operated the main gate. To the right of the main entrance, closer to the main road and nestled up to the final curve of the driveway, sat the tower. It was a strategic location, permitting the tower guard to look out over a key curve in the driveway and out to the main road.

But being in the tower was mind-numbingly boring, because there was so little traffic entering the base. An occasional fuel truck and perhaps a couple of sedans would arrive, Foster recalled, but it was usually quiet for hours at a time.

When they weren't on guard duty, Foster and his buddies exercised . . . a *lot*. Working out became a passion, largely because there was nothing else to do. "I was getting pretty big," Foster said. The guys had commandeered an open space in the barracks and created a small gym area, with emphasis on the word "small." "If you had four people in there," Foster said, "it was getting pretty packed." They had makeshift weights, improvised from anything they could lay their hands on to whatever gear they could swipe from bases nearby. Some even purchased equipment and nutritional products online and had it shipped to them at the base. "You'd get a mail run and you'd get maybe twenty to thirty letters out of it," Foster recalled, "and then one hundred boxes of weightlifting supplements."

But doing bench presses with homemade weights was not what they wanted to do. They wanted *action*. And in their isolated, inconsequential patrol station, they were getting no action at all. The inaction was particularly galling because the rest of their company, sitting only twenty miles away, was getting loads of combat experience. Starting in March 2010, roughly a month into their deployment, Foster's platoon heard reports that their sister units were receiving mortar fire virtually every day and engaging with enemy forces on a weekly—and sometimes daily—basis. Foster's unit frequently mobilized to support their brethren, but the firefights always ended before they arrived. Foster recalled how guys from his platoon would drive to the company's base every few weeks for supplies, and they would hear about their comrades' combat experiences. "You would see the guys you've been training with for the past couple of years, and you haven't done *anything*, and they're saying 'We just got shot up,' or 'We take thirty mortar rounds a day,'" Foster said with mounting irritation in his voice. "Most of us *hated* where we were. It felt like we weren't doing a thing there—just like our first deployment. It was *way* too comfy to be a war."

That boredom endured for months and months. But it would end abruptly in the early morning hours of May 21, 2010.

Around midnight on that night, Foster was on guard duty up in the tower. It was a typical overnight shift—not much happening. His rotation had started two hours earlier and was slated to end at 6:00 that morning. As Foster was going through his list of preplanned contemplations, an American supply convoy comprising hundreds of vehicles passed by their station on the paved road. A mile down the road from their base, insurgents ambushed the convoy. "We could see the hill that they're getting shot from," Foster recalled. "We could see the flashes and the trucks returning fire." It was a brief skirmish—the convoy took no casualties and promptly resumed its trek. Foster's unit never mobilized in support.

After watching the flare-up, Foster was livid. "*Motherfucker,*" he muttered to himself, "I bet they were coming for *us.*" They had been foiled yet again. "It was only a mile away. We're *never* gonna get respect here." After the convoy left, the night returned to its typical boring nothingness—a couple of passing vehicles here and there, but nothing important.

By 5:45 that morning, roughly six hours after the convoy's firefight, Foster was ready to get down from the tower. He slumped languidly on one of the sandbag piles, bored as usual. He had exhausted that night's thinking list and was listening to his iPod, which blasted "Locked Up" by Akon in his right ear. He and the other two men had already called for the next shift.

Then Foster heard pop . . . pop . . . pop . . . pop. It was gunfire, roiling the predawn stillness. The shots came from the main road. They were not sporadic or spraying; the gun was firing in a deliberate, rhythmic pattern with a momentary pause in between. He radioed to Robinson, his buddy down at the gate, to see what he thought. Neither was particularly concerned, as the shots were not directed at them or the base. So they shrugged their shoulders and did not think much about it.

That changed a moment later, when a mammoth supply vehicle, roughly the size of a construction dump truck, turned from the main road into the base's dirt driveway. This was odd—not necessarily alarming, but certainly out of the ordinary. A truck like that would rarely, if ever, come into the base, except perhaps as part of a two-hundred-vehicle supply convoy. And such a delivery would have been scheduled far in advance, would have been listed on the log at the gate, and definitely would not be scheduled for 5:45 in the morning. Although the truck struck him as unusual, Foster was not sure it was an enemy vehicle. They could be civilians veering off the road to avoid the gunfire Foster had heard a few moments earlier.

Foster squinted his eyes to look into the truck, which was sitting about forty meters away at the end of the driveway. He could make out two men. They had short beards, and the driver was a bit heavier than the passenger. Foster gave them the benefit of the doubt at that point—he desperately wanted to avoid a repeat of the shooting debacle of a few weeks earlier.

His hackles rose, however, when the truck started moving down the driveway toward the base. Foster counted to three to make sure they were not innocent civilians. The truck slowed as it descended into the ditch by the main road. Then Foster heard its engine roar. "When I saw them hit that dip and heard them hit the gas and rev the engine, I was on the bolt of the machine gun," Foster said. "As soon as he hit the gas and came forward, I squeezed the trigger—I put at least thirty to forty rounds in the windshield."

His rounds tore through the truck. "They were about thirty meters away. I saw the glass explode. It was just like you see in the action movies—the bodies riddling back against the seat, and they just slumped forward," Foster recalled. There was a moment of eerie silence. "The truck stopped, and then *nothing* happened."

Foster leaned out through the window of the tower, looking down at the truck. It had rolled to a stop about fifteen meters from the tower. It sat essentially straight in front of the tower, outside the base's inner wall and perpendicular to the base. "The first thing I thought was that my commander would be pissed because I shot these civilians. All I could think is, 'I am going to get fuckin' screamed at for this one,'" Foster recalled. "I remember thinking, 'I'm in *trouble*. Goddamn it, not *again*.'"

As he peered down at the motionless truck and his mind filled with dread about the looming discipline, the truck detonated. "I saw a small orange flash and a big orange flash," Foster recalled. The explosion wrenched him backward, knocking him violently to the ground. Suddenly, he recalled, "I was on my ass staring up in the tower." He was shaken and, although he stayed conscious, he was quite discombobulated. The billowing smoke and debris from the explosion cast a dense haze throughout the room, choking his lungs and clouding his vision. His hearing was little better; he could make out some noises in the background, but his ears were ringing badly. Everything sounded like "a loud, fuzzy hum," he said, "almost like machinery at a factory—static noise."

Foster tried to clear his foggy mind and figure out what was going on. He opened the door on the side of the tower to clear the swirling smoke and sand. He stepped out onto the steep ladder adjacent to the tower, so that he could get a breath of fresh air and get a sense of the situation.

As the smoke cleared, Foster saw rockets streaking in the air and started to realize what was happening: they were under attack.

Out on the ladder, seeing rocket streaks in the air and hearing mortar rounds explode nearby, Foster recognized that he was in trouble. His brain was still hazy—"it was still not quite clicking"—but he understood that he was completely exposed out on the ladder. "It wasn't the smartest place to stand," Foster said. "I didn't want to get shot on the ledge, like an idiot." So he scampered back into the tower and slammed the door behind him.

Back in the tower, he gave himself a once-over to see whether he was injured. "I checked my arms real quickly and my legs. I didn't see anything. I was still moving, so I said to myself, 'I'm fine,'" he recalled. "I was still feeling pretty good at this point." He heard his buddy Nick Robinson down at the gate say over the radio that he was taking fire from all sides, including mortars, and that he needed backup. Foster, still cloudy and not quite grasping the extent of the attack, radioed back that it was just a truck bomb and that he had stopped it.

Looking down on the scene from the tower, Foster saw two individuals start walking toward the base from the driveway. One was about five foot ten and skinny, while the other guy had a light beard. They were both wearing American uniforms, but they were carrying AK-47s. This confused him even further. "It was really weird," Foster recalled, because those were the weapons of choice for insurgents, not Americans or NATO personnel. But he had previously trained with some Afghan troops that were using those rifles, so it was not totally unprecedented. Plus, Foster's mind was still "pretty fuzzy," and in those cloudy moments, he was still trying to wrap his head around the events. "I couldn't put two and two together still," he recalled. He asked himself, "Who the fuck are these guys?!"

The men proceed toward the main gate. Foster recalled vividly the way the men walked—they were *strutting*. "They had this look on them, like they could fuck up *anything*," he said. "They had a look when they came in like the look you get when you know you're going to win—you know you're *golden*." One of the outsiders, as he approached the gate, turned his AK-47 toward two Afghan guards who had joined Robinson in defending the gate. He was two feet away from the Afghan soldiers. Without changing his pace or even facing the targets, the strutting man shot at the Afghan guards. "He squeezed the trigger," Foster recalled, "and just hosed them down." It should have been a Mafia-style, point-blank execution, but he was evidently a bad shot—he hit one guard in the neck, but missed the other completely.

The shooting jarred Foster out of his funk. "That's when everything sort of clicked back in for me, and I fully understood the situation." He grabbed the Mark 48 machine gun. "I saw that [shooting], and I was already behind the [machine gun] and I squeezed the trigger—pa-pa-pa-pa-pa-pa! I hit one, and I remember seeing the look on his face as soon as he heard the machine gun, like sheer, 'I fucked up' terror," Foster said. "It was *awesome*." That episode—wiping the insurgent's smug look off his face and replacing it with sheer terror—would be one of Foster's favorite moments of that day.

His elation ended quickly. After the gun fired off six or seven shots, enough to cut down the two strutters, Foster heard a sound that all infantry soldiers dread—it was the loud metallic clang of his gun misfiring. Then he heard the bolt of the gun slam forward, and the Mark 48 fell silent. "That," Foster said, "was a fucked-up moment."

He dropped down to the ground, where the ammunition lay, and saw that the links of the ammunition belt lay in tatters. So he grabbed a bunch of loose rounds and threw them in the gun. He stood up, engaged the bolt, and looked out the window for something to shoot.

There were plenty of targets.

Insurgents swarmed around him. They also surrounded Robinson's position at the gate. Teams of insurgents were also holed up in buildings on the other side of the main road, launching mortars and rocket-propelled grenades in support of the guerrillas near the gate.

But Foster was mostly concerned about the insurgents essentially at his doorstep—he could see six guerrillas surrounding the tower, three on his left and three on his right. They were only twenty to thirty meters away. "It wasn't far at all," he said. They were dressed in traditional Afghan clothes, except they were also crisscrossed with bags of ammunition and gun harnesses. "Most looked like standard farmers, except for the magazine pouches."

They were hiding behind the giant Hescos and shooting up at him in the tower. Although some fired wildly, simply sticking the guns above the Hescos and aimlessly spraying in the direction of the tower, others were shooting accurately. "You could see the flashes. You could feel them crack off the tower," Foster said. "Every time a round came anywhere close to you, you hear a crack as it goes by, splitting the air. You hear that, and you hear it echo as it impacted in the tower. You could feel the concrete off the tower shattering behind you—tat!-tat!-tat!-tat!-tat!" The impact of the bullets, compounded by the reverberating echo within the tiny concrete room, was deafening. "It sounded like someone was hitting a hammer against a rock of concrete as hard as they could." He also compared it to a firecracker exploding in a can, except *much* louder.

There was nowhere for Foster to hide, so he dove down below the window opening and wedged himself in the sandbags piled on the ground. He waited until the shooting stopped and then—despite being outnumbered, surrounded, and exposed—he stood up behind the Mark 48 to fire back.

Foster tried to be judicious with his fire, waiting until the guerrillas stood up, not just until they stuck out the barrels of their rifles. He also targeted the insurgents at the Hescos, rather than insurgents across the road, because they were trying to push forward into the base. "I was engaged with the closest targets at that point, so I wasn't worried about the people in the houses." His hands tingled as he pulled the trigger and felt the ammunition feed into the gun. Plumes of smoke and sand puffed from the Hescos as his rounds slammed into the huge containers.

After a well-placed burst of ten to twenty rounds, Foster saw the insurgents' guns come back from behind the Hescos and take aim at him again. He ducked down below the window, and the cacophonous symphony of shattering concrete erupted around him once again. The splintering concrete threw incredible dust in the air, which mixed with the smoke from Foster's Mark 48 and the debris from the initial explosion. It became so cloudy that he could not breathe. "It was better when you could stand up and shoot back because you could breathe."

Foster traded fire with the insurgents in this manner several times, each side ducking behind cover when the enemy sent volleys of fire and then popping up to return fire. His Mark 48 devoured ammunition—Foster whipped through an entire belt containing hundreds of bullets and, during one of his defensive crouches, had to load in another belt. It was something out of an action movie, Foster recalled.

Despite the danger, Foster did not panic. "There was not a lot going through my mind at this point—I wasn't thinking about the situation," he said. "I wasn't scared of the guys, and I wasn't scared of the attack. I just didn't want to get shot. I don't remember really breathing heavy at that point," he said. In fact, Foster actually enjoyed the fight to some degree. "It was kind of like a game."

As Foster and Robinson staved off the approaching guerrillas, their unit began waking up and responding to the attack. Within minutes, one of Foster's buddies came up the tower ladder, yelling: "Friendly comin' up!" He opened the door to the tower and dropped a couple of cans of ammunition inside the little room.

Looking up, the soldier saw Foster and froze. The man had a startled, "blank-eyed" look, Foster recalled, as if he were in shock and completely unaware that they were in a firefight. His look said: "What the fuck happened to you?"

Foster looked around the tower room and, for the first time, appreciated the scene and why his comrade was startled. The room was a frenzied mess, with smoke and dust choking the air, chunks of concrete peppered throughout the floor, and bullet casings strewn around. Worse, blood—*Foster's* blood—was splattered all over. Foster had not realized that he was injured at this point, except for some annoying grittiness in his mouth. But his buddy was clearly taken aback at Foster's appearance. Regardless, Foster was feeling no pain at the moment and grabbed his comrade by the shoulder and threw him on the Mark 48. The two men then acted as a gun team, alternating their duties—picking out targets, lubricating the gun with gun oil from a nearby stash, and then manning the gun.

After a few minutes, the platoon medic came out running toward the tower and hollered at Foster from the bottom of the stairs to come down. Foster scurried down the steep ladder, eager to tell the doc that he had killed two of the insurgents. "I was fucking ecstatic," he recalled, about shooting the two strutting insurgents. He was having difficulty talking, so he pantomimed the number two, pointed to his chest, and then made a chopping-head motion with his finger. But when Foster saw the medic's reaction to his face, he knew there was a problem. "As soon as I got there, he looked at me and gave me this wrinkled face, this 'What the fuck happened to you?' look." The medic instructed him to run back to the base's medical room because his injuries needed treatment.

As he ran back to the base's main building, he spotted a couple of buddies in a truck heading toward the insurgent attack. Foster could not resist telling his buddies about his exploits. "I'm waving my arms out, pointing the number two, trying to tell them that I shot two people. 'I got *two*! Over *there*!'"

In the main building, on his way to the medical room, Foster retrieved a shotgun from his room and grabbed a fistful of shells. Waiting for the medic to arrive, he loaded the shotgun and prepared to go back out to the fight.

In the base's cramped medical room, the platoon medic worked hard to patch up Foster's face and mouth. At first, the rush of combat dulled his pain. "That's when I noticed the adrenaline was in me. Nothing could go wrong," he said. "I was in pretty happy spirits, laughing about everything." He cracked a few jokes, saying he was going to look like one of their squad leaders, who had problems with his teeth.

As the medic continued to work on his face and mouth, however, Foster started to appreciate just how serious his injuries were. The doc was wrapping up his wounds with thick gauze, going deep in his mouth. He pulled out a bucket for Foster to lean over and let the blood pour out of his mouth. He told Foster that his face, from the tip of his nose to his upper lip, was sliced in half and that the rest of his upper lip had been shredded. The bones in his face had suffered serious trauma. He saw that several teeth were missing, and a few of the remaining teeth were hanging out of his mouth.

"At that point, I was getting feeling back, and I could feel what he was talking about," Foster said. He looked in a mirror and thought his face looked "like a plate of really bad food." It was far worse than the chipped tooth he initially felt. "An open patch of my mouth was gone and there were jagged shards of teeth." The left side of his mouth was particularly annoying because half of a tooth had been sheared off, and the rest remained jammed in his gumline. He could not feel it and it did not hurt, but he could not stop touching it. "It was driving me *insane*. I was trying to suck it out and pull it out, and I couldn't do it. *That is what was buggin' me—that fuckin' tooth!*"

But his injuries were far more severe than an annoying tooth. The medic made it clear that Foster was going home.

Dan Foster

Despite his injuries, Foster was not done fighting. After the medic left to take care of soldiers who were in more critical condition, Foster grabbed his shotgun and tried to help out his buddies. A sergeant asked him to help find the platoon medic, so Foster stood up to find him. "By the time I got out the door," Foster said, "I wasn't wearing any gear—just pants, boots, T-shirt, and a shotgun—running through the open area in the base, with RPG trails streaking the air."

Later, Foster heard a call for ammunition from the tower and made another two trips—again without any protective gear—to secure additional rounds for the guys on the guns. On the second trip, he began running to take an ammo load to the tower, which was fifty yards away. To get to the tower, Foster would have to cross an exposed area in the middle of the base, which was receiving effective enemy fire and mortar rounds from enemy positions.

Before he could get very far, however, one of the platoon sergeants told him to stay back and get treatment. He kneeled outside the main building of the base, waiting for the medic to return from treating other injured men. As he waited, other insurgents popped up on a mountainside overlooking the base, situated roughly two hundred yards away, and started taking pot shots at the troops in the base. Foster, with no helmet or body armor and only a twelve-gauge shotgun, could not resist the temptation to fight and started shooting back at them. "I knew I didn't have a prayer in hell of hitting them," he said, noting that the insurgents were far outside the shotgun's range. But he blasted a few shots anyway, hoping to take some pressure off the rest of his platoon.

About an hour after the initial truck-bomb explosion, a helicopter arrived to evacuate Foster and other wounded troops to a medical facility. Foster felt like a sitting duck in the aircraft. "As the helicopter took off, you could hear rifle cracks below," he said. "That was the only time I felt afraid during all that. I don't know what it was, but you look down, and you feel really vulnerable sitting in that helicopter, hearing the bullets going underneath and you're thinking, 'Oh my God—I'm going to get shot in this stupid fucking helicopter, after this whole fuckin' thing. What a shitty way to go.'"

He was eventually evacuated to the battalion base, which lay four miles away. The medics there, who were friends from Fort Campbell, administered huge doses of morphine to blunt the increasing pain. To understand the full extent of his injuries, the doctors needed full-body x-rays, which meant that Foster had to drop his pants in front of a room full of people. With the morphine working its magic on his brain, Foster dropped his pants—wearing nothing underneath—and danced a little shimmy for his audience.

Foster endured multiple surgeries and intensive care units over the ensuing weeks. Over the course of his treatment, he learned that he had lost thirteen teeth and substantial bone structure from his upper and lower jaws. The surgeries left a three-inch scar on his face, and most of his upper lip was scar tissue. He also suffered some brain trauma, which has impacted his speech patterns. "I stutter a little more now, and I'll be talking to people and—midsentence—I'll forget what I was saying." The blast from the initial truck bomb, not to mention the thunderous clamor echoing throughout the tower room during the firefight, damaged his hearing. "I can't hear [anything] out of my left ear. But my right ear, though, has damn good hearing because the earbud was in it. Akon saved my hearing," he said. All told, Foster said, his injuries were "not too bad."

After weeks of treatment in Afghanistan and Germany, he was eventually transferred back to Fort Campbell, where he reunited with his family for the first time since the injury. He was nervous about seeing them, particularly his mother, sister, and girlfriend. "I definitely looked different," he said, "so I just wanted to make sure they knew I was okay." It was good to be home, although their reunion involved a substantial amount of tears. "A bunch of crybabies," he said with a chuckle.

❧

Foster was honored with a Silver Star and a Purple Heart for his actions on May 21, 2010. He was proud of the Purple Heart, calling it a badge of honor. He viewed the Silver Star completely differently. In his mind, his actions did not rise to the level of an honor like the Silver Star. "I didn't feel like I'd earned it because my buddies would have done the same thing," he said. "I was just in the right place at the right time."

He also felt the Silver Star was a bit showy, running counter to the Army culture of teamwork over individuality. "In the Army, you never flaunted your awards. There are tons more people who have gotten hurt and done greater things than I've done and didn't get any awards," he said. "I still don't bring it up to people. I still haven't come to terms with it myself."

So, when the Army notified him that he had been awarded a Silver Star and asked about his preferences for the presentation ceremony, Foster wanted to avoid a big, ostentatious event. He responded that they should mail it to him. But the Army pushed back. So Foster tried to think of a request that was too over the top and would undoubtedly get rejected. "Where is the *last* place that they'd do the ceremony?" he asked himself. He finally thought of something truly untenable: opening night at Angel Stadium. "It was the most extreme thing I could find," he said. "I thought there is *no way* they'll do this for me. Then they called me back ten minutes later and said: 'Okay, no problem.' I responded: "Uh. *What?!*"

On April 9, 2011, in a ceremony before a crowd of thousands at a Los Angeles Angels' game, Foster received a Silver Star. At Foster's request, the Army flew in roughly a dozen of his buddies for the event, including Nick Robinson, the guard at the gate. Foster said that Robinson, who had also received a Silver Star for his actions in that engagement, certainly deserves the honor: "That dude was a little badass that day." In fact, Foster credited Robinson with almost single-handedly saving the base from the insurgent attack. "He handled himself very well."

Although Foster was a tad nervous about the presentation ceremony, he was excited to see his buddies for the first time in a while. "We were more happy to see each other and hang out than [about the] award." But the ceremony ended up being special for Foster. As the speaker read what he had done, the fans cheered so loud that no one could hear the second half of the speech. "It felt good," Foster admitted. "It was pretty humbling."

Looking back on the firefight and his tenure in the Army, Foster feels that he did accomplish something. Still, he does not feel that he belongs in the same echelon as his World War II heroes. "I don't feel like one of those men," he said. "I put them on a pedestal that I don't know if I can reach. But after going through it all, I don't think those men put themselves on it either. I believe they put all their comrades up there, but not themselves. Even talking with buddies now, each one of us puts each other higher than ourselves based on injuries or experience. I have friends that have taken bullets—that have had plenty more firefights than me—but put me higher above them for whatever reason. I'm jealous of all my buddies who finished the deployment, feeling they did far more than I ever did. I may not walk as tall as those men walking out of the forests, but I walk plenty tall standing next to my brothers who went to their own hell and back."

About the Author

Mark Lee Greenblatt is an attorney based in the Washington, D.C., area who specializes in criminal and ethics investigations. Mark is involved in several community service activities, including serving as vice president of the Marian Greenblatt Education Fund, a foundation created in honor of his mother to honor excellence in education. He received his undergraduate degree from Duke University and his law degree from Columbia University. He was also a Senior Managers in Government Fellow at the Kennedy School of Government at Harvard University. Mark has earned a black belt in tae kwon do and was the drummer in The Fiasco, widely considered the greatest rock-and-roll band since The Beatles. He lives with his wife and two sons in Bethesda, Maryland.